CW00673038

To

_____

From

_____

Date

_____

ONE-MINUTE DEVOTIONS

DAILY HABITS
OF THE
Heart

KATHERINE BUTLER

Christian art gifts®

Visit Christian Art Gifts website at www.christianartgifts.com.

Daily Habits of the Heart

Published by Christian Art Gifts, Inc.

Previously published as Habits of the Heart: 365 Daily Exercises for Living like Jesus. First printing by Tyndale House Publishers in 2017.

Daily Habits of the Heart © 2021 by Katherine J. Butler. All rights reserved.

Designed by Allison Sowers

Cover and interior images used under license from Shutterstock.com.

ISBN 978-1-64272-847-7

Printed in China

26 25 24 23 22 21

10 9 8 7 6 5 4 3 2 1

CONTENTS

WEEK 9: *Becoming Teachable*

Being a lifelong learner, with the Lord as your teacher and guide.

WEEK 10: *Learning Discernment*

Learning to better recognize God's voice and becoming more sensitive to His direction in your life.

WEEK 11: *Choosing Joy*

Making a conscious decision to develop an attitude of appreciation, thanksgiving, and rejoicing—regardless of circumstances.

WEEK 12: *Practicing Conversational Prayer*

Bringing every thought and feeling to God in prayer.

WEEK 13: *Caring for Yourself*

Making time to care for your heart, mind, and body—all of which make up the soul.

WEEK 14: *Serving Others*

Intentionally recognizing the needs around you and then meeting them.

WEEK 15: *Welcoming Silence*

Creating quiet space in your noisy, chaotic days to hear from God more clearly.

WEEK 16: *Offering Worship*

Recognizing God's great work and gifts in your life and responding by giving Him the praise and glory He deserves.

WEEK 17: *Living in Contentment*

Being at peace with how God made you, where He has placed you, what He has given you, and who you are in relation to Him.

WEEK 18: *Practicing Generosity*

Giving freely and joyfully of your time, possessions, talents, and money.

WEEK 19: *Keeping an Eternal Perspective*

Living on earth with eternity in mind.

WEEK 20: *Being Steadfast*

Cultivating an enduring and patient trust in God's faithfulness.

WEEK 21: *Unplugging*

Detaching from routine distractions, especially technology, to be fully present with God and others.

WEEK 22: *Being Present*

Awakening to the world around you so you don't miss the gifts God has for you in the moment.

WEEK 23: *Listening*

Letting others know they are loved and valuable by paying full attention to what they say and showing them respect, care, and patience.

WEEK 24: *Practicing Thoughtfulness*

Being considerate and attentive to the feelings, needs, and situations of others.

WEEK 25: *Controlling Your Tongue*

Growing in awareness of what comes out of your mouth and then, with the power of the Holy Spirit, changing hurtful words into those that are gracious, grateful, encouraging, loving, truthful, and a blessing to others.

WEEK 26: *Praying for Others*

Coming before the Lord on behalf of another.

WEEK 27: *Developing a Heart of Compassion*

Opening your heart to the hurt around you and then doing something about it.

WEEK 28: *Being in Fellowship*

Exemplifying God's nature as you do life together with your brothers and sisters in the church.

WEEK 29: *Caring for Creation*

Seeing all of what God has made as "good" and then working to be a good steward over it.

WEEK 30: *Living Simply*

Letting go of things that clutter and complicate your life in order to keep your focus on Jesus.

WEEK 31: *Meditating on God's Word*

Deeply pondering God's Word and what it reveals about Him.

WEEK 32: *Keeping Sabbath*

Setting aside one day a week to embrace rest so that you have space to worship and enjoy God.

WEEK 33: *Trusting in God*

Believing that God loves you, that He's absolutely good, and that He wants and is able to do good things in your life.

WEEK 34: *Witnessing*

Telling others about your experience of how you grew to know and love Jesus.

WEEK 35: *Making a Sacrifice*

Relinquishing something you think you need or that makes you feel secure in order to rely on God to provide what He knows you need.

WEEK 36: *Incorporating Prayer Postures*

Using your body in prayer to move your heart toward a place of humility, boldness, submission, gratitude, reverence, and worship.

WEEK 37: *Accepting Solitude*

Intentionally stepping away from normal human interaction in order to grow in your friendship with the Lord.

WEEK 38: *Hoping in God*

Choosing confident joy in the face of uncertainty as you trust God with your present and future.

WEEK 39: *Waiting Well*

Using your seasons of waiting to learn to walk with God in patience and hope and resisting the urge to rush ahead of His timing.

WEEK 40: *Using Imaginative Prayer*

Actively engaging your mind and heart in prayer by placing yourself in a scene in Scripture through the use of your imagination.

WEEK 41: *Keeping Secrets*

Keeping certain things between you and God.

WEEK 42: *Developing Hospitality*

Becoming a safe person and cultivating space for others to experience the welcoming presence of God.

WEEK 43: *Praying Scripture*

Reading the prayers in the Bible as your own.

WEEK 44: *Being Frugal*

Choosing to live below your means to be free from wants (and debts!) that would otherwise distract you from effectively knowing and serving God.

WEEK 45: *Resting*

Making time in your everyday life to intentionally restore your mind, body, and soul.

WEEK 46: *Guarding Your Heart*

Learning to be more alert to temptation and then guarding your heart from giving in to it.

WEEK 47: *Practicing Gratitude*

Staying connected to God by thanking Him—no matter what life has in store for you today.

WEEK 48: *Letting Go*

Releasing your grip on things in this world that have come to replace your need for and trust in God.

WEEK 49: *Celebrating*

Opening up your heart to delight in, be thankful for, and fully enjoy God and the life He has offered you.

WEEK 50: *Memorizing Scripture*

Allowing God's Word to shape your mind and heart through repetition and reflection.

WEEK 51: *Reflecting on the Past Year*

Pausing to reflect on how God worked in and around you this past year.

WEEK 52: *Looking Forward to the New Year*

Pausing to reflect on how God might be leading you as you enter into the new year.

INTRODUCTION

Do You Long for Lasting Change?

———— ♥ ————

If you want to change your life, you have to do something different. Lasting change comes only from developing new habits. A "habit" is a *routine of behavior that a person repeats regularly and usually unconsciously.*

Many of us try to make physical exercise a daily habit. Or perhaps we want to become good at playing a musical instrument, so we get into the habit of practicing every day. If we want to graduate from college, we need the habit of regular study. *Developing a habit is really a way of training our bodies or minds to behave differently so often that it becomes routine.*

Many of us don't think about training our hearts, but the truth is, we train them every day. When we watch a TV show, we are training our hearts. When we focus on lies instead of truth, we are training our hearts. When we choose to pray instead of worry, we are training our hearts. The apostle Paul tells us that our whole lives are a training of some sort, whether we realize it or not: Everything we do is training our hearts either toward God or away from Him. When our hearts are conditioned to discern the Spirit of God and act upon what He wants, then we experience the greatest possible joy, peace, and satisfaction. It is essential that we develop the habit of "exercising" our hearts in the practice of godliness.

What shape is your heart in? Consider this book a training program to develop habits of the heart that will draw you into a deep and lasting relationship with God. This simple guide focuses on one essential aspect each week and provides daily exercises to make it become a habit. Each day begins with Scripture, followed by a question to prayerfully consider with the Lord or a spiritual exercise that calls you to put God's Word into action. The exercises are based entirely on Scripture and Jesus' life and teachings. Over the next year, you will be introduced to fifty-two spiritual disciplines that will connect you with God in new ways. The goal is to recognize the places where you currently live apart from God so that you can prayerfully invite Him into all your daily moments. That is the beginning of real transformation.

A FEW GUIDELINES TO CONSIDER

Be open. What does it mean to "be open to God"? It means having a posture that is ready to receive. For example, if someone throws you a baseball, you need a posture to catch it. This requires not only having your hands out and open to receive the ball but also paying attention to the one who throws it. To keep yourself open to God, as you work through each devotion, ask Him, "What do you want to teach me from this?" Some exercises may seem pointless and silly. Can listening to music, enjoying flavorful foods, driving in the slow lane, or using your imagination really be part of your spiritual transformation? Yes, they can! Anything that draws you toward God can be "devotional." Be open to the variety of ways God may teach you, trusting the Holy Spirit is in control.

Be patient. Spiritual exercises are not quick fixes to make you a "good" Christian. They are meant to *slowly* open and shape your heart to become more like Jesus. There is no right way to do these exercises. If, in a particular week, you feel you've failed to grow, that area may be one where growth is occurring more subtly. Just as your body is made up of many muscles, so it is with the soul. Feeling resistance is a sign a spiritual muscle needs to be strengthened. God may also use an exercise to show you something about yourself that you find difficult to accept. Remember, the only way he can transform your heart to be more like his is to first show you the places where you aren't like Him. Learn to see this as a gift because God is showing you something that is keeping you from fully trusting and loving Him.

Be expectant. God is active in the world and present in your everyday life. You have the very power of God inside you! As you go through this devotional, wake up each morning anticipating that the Holy Spirit is doing great work within your heart. The fact that you have picked up this book is evidence that God is already at work. Keep a journal to record your thoughts and prayers, frequently looking back and reflecting on your journey. May God bless you as He uses His Word to challenge and change you to be more like Jesus.

WEEK 1

JAN. 1

Look Again. Can You See Me Now?

♥

If you look for Me wholeheartedly, you will find Me.
JEREMIAH 29:13

The Bible tells many stories of people who were in the very presence of God but were completely unaware of it. Jacob was camping overnight, for instance, when he realized he had missed God trying to communicate with him and exclaimed, "Surely the LORD is in this place, and I wasn't even aware of it!" (Genesis 28:16). Jesus' own disciples didn't recognize they were walking with Him on the road to Emmaus (Luke 24:13-16).

What causes you to miss God's presence and activity in your day? Practicing God's presence is about awakening a constant attentiveness to God always being with you, working on your behalf. As you develop this awareness, worry, discouragement, and fear will lose their power over you.

This book intentionally begins with "Practicing God's Presence" because this sets the stage for the rest of the year. As you work through each devotion, remember God is with you in every moment. Don't miss what He is doing right in front of you!

I Am with You

♥

The LORD your God is living among you. He is a mighty savior.
He will take delight in you with gladness. With His love, He will
calm all your fears. He will rejoice over you with joyful songs.

ZEPHANIAH 3:17

I am with you always.

MATTHEW 28:20

Because of Christ and our faith in Him, we can now
come boldly and confidently into God's presence.

EPHESIANS 3:12

Set an alarm on your phone or place a note in your home as a simple
reminder that God is with you and delights in you. When you see
the reminder, pause for a few moments and say to Him, "Thank
You for taking delight in me, even though sometimes I have a
difficult time accepting that. Help me to remember throughout
this day that You are by my side in each and every moment."

Open Your Eyes

♥

I can never escape from Your Spirit! I can never get away
from Your presence! If I go up to heaven, You are there;
if I go down to the grave, You are there. If I ride the wings
of the morning, if I dwell by the farthest oceans, even there
Your hand will guide me, and Your strength will support me.

PSALM 139:7–10

How easy is it for God to get your attention throughout the day?
In *Letters to Malcolm: Chiefly on Prayer*, C. S. Lewis wrote, "We may
ignore, but we can nowhere evade, the presence of God. The world
is crowded with Him. He walks everywhere *incognito*."[1]

Look for His presence all around you today in ways you hadn't
thought about before (through the comfort of another person, a
beautiful sunset, a song on the radio, or a Scripture that comes
to mind).

Let Me Come with You

♥

This is My command—be strong and courageous! Do not be afraid or discouraged. For the LORD your God is with you wherever you go.
JOSHUA 1:9

I know the LORD is always with me.
I will not be shaken, for He is right beside me.
PSALM 16:8

Imagine God speaking these words directly to you: "Do not be afraid … I am with you wherever you go."

How might this encourage you in the transitions you currently face (such as moving to a new home, starting a different job, experiencing a child's move out of the house)?

Memorize one of the above Scriptures to remind you that God is with you right now and will continue to be with you every day for the rest of your life.

JAN. 5

Let Go to Focus on Me

♥

The Lord said to her, "My dear Martha, you are worried and upset over
all these details! There is only one thing worth being concerned about.
Mary has discovered it, and it will not be taken away from her."

LUKE 10:41–42

What details in your day distract you from being present with
Jesus?

Make a list of these disruptions and talk to the Lord about each
of them. Ask Him to make His presence more urgent to you than
your distractions.

When you are done talking to God about your list, place your
Bible on top of the list to symbolize letting those things go for
today in order to focus on being more present with Him.

Remember Me

♥

Commit yourselves wholeheartedly to these commands....
Repeat them again and again.... Talk about them when you are at
home and when you are on the road, when you are going to bed and
when you are getting up.... Write them on the doorposts of your house.

DEUTERONOMY 6:6–9

I know the LORD is always with me.
I will not be shaken, for He is right beside me.

PSALM 16:8

Every time you remember God's faithfulness, your trust in His love and care for you grows stronger. Today, carry something with you that can remind you of God's constant presence.

For example, wear a special bracelet, place a token in your pocket, or put your Bible in a visible spot in your home or office. Whenever you see this item, thank God for never leaving your side.

I Follow You with Blessing

♥

You go before me and follow me.
You place Your hand of blessing on my head.
PSALM 139:5

God does not want you to go through this day alone. As you think through the things you need to do, close your eyes and picture God's hand on your head.

What blessing is He speaking over your day?

Write out that blessing and carry it with you throughout today as a tangible reminder to encourage you.

At the end of the day, come back to this page and consider these questions:

- When did you feel close to God in the past week?
- What exercises helped you remember God's presence with you?
- How can you make practicing God's presence a habit?

WEEK 2

JAN. 8

Why the Hurry?

♥

> He lets me rest in green meadows;
> He leads me beside peaceful streams.
> **PSALM 23:2**

In a culture that praises a hurried lifestyle, we are tempted to believe constant activity is fulfilling and important. But hurrying doesn't allow us to go deep, and thus it diminishes our ability to do things well.

God did not intend for us to race through the only life we have been given. If we did, we would miss those significant moments God wants us to enjoy or learn from.

The practice of *slowing down* is about resisting the need to always look toward the next thing. Slowing down replaces trust in our own speed and control with trust in God's timing and control.

As you begin to practice slowing down, you may experience anxiety, unease, or irritation. Pause and talk to the Lord about those feelings. Your heart and mind will need more than a week to *really* slow down, but this week will introduce you to the discipline of a life that is unhurried, peaceful, and "in the moment."

Just Breathe

How do you know what your life will be like tomorrow?
Your life is like the morning fog—it's here a little while, then it's gone.
JAMES 4:14

Get into a comfortable position. Allow your body to relax, and notice where you hold your tension. Close your eyes and breathe in slowly, allowing your breath to fill your lungs completely.

As you inhale, thank God for the gift of life, and for His breath that gave life to all creation. When you breathe out slowly, imagine exhaling your stress, anxiety, and tension. Do this several more times. Finish by thanking God for the gift of His life-giving breath in your lungs.

Then think about how you can slow down today to be more present with God. For the rest of this week, commit to begin each day's devotion with this breathing exercise.

No Rush

♥

Be still, and know that I am God!
PSALM 46:10

Jesus said, "Come to me, all of you who are weary and
carry heavy burdens, and I will give you rest. Take My yoke
upon you. Let me teach you, because I am humble and
gentle at heart, and you will find rest for your souls."
MATTHEW 11:28-29

To build your trust that God is in control, choose one activity to help you resist unnecessary hurry: walk slower, don't rush through a conversation, avoid multitasking, leave five minutes early, or let go of items on your to-do list.

Pray, "Lord, please make me aware today when I'm going too fast. Show me how to let go of my need to control my schedule. Help me to allow You to control my time instead. Teach me to resist hurry so that I can lean into You today."

Just a Moment

❤

LORD, remind me how brief my time on earth will be.
Remind me that my days are numbered—how fleeting
my life is. You have made my life no longer than the
width of my hand. My entire lifetime is just a moment
to You; at best, each of us is but a breath. We are merely
moving shadows, and all our busy rushing ends in nothing.
PSALM 39:4-6

Read the passage above again, but this time do it *slowly*. What did
you miss the first time? What does this show you about how you
read Scripture?

Now, *slowly* write down the Scripture and meditate on the
words. What might God be saying to you through His Word?

Linger at the Table

---♥---

Taste and see that the LORD is good.
Oh, the joys of those who take refuge in Him!

PSALM 34:8

Someone once said, "There is a special bond of fellowship when people linger at the table around good food. Among Jesus followers, it becomes much like a Holy Communion." Consider these words and what they mean as you eat each meal today.

Set a note on your kitchen table (or wherever you eat) to remind you to chew your food slowly. Sit at the table if you usually eat on the couch or in front of the TV. Linger at the table longer than you normally would. Take time to smell, taste, and enjoy your food.

Allow this exercise to remind you how slowing down helps you better appreciate God's gifts in the moment.

Cherish the "Lasts"

♥

Teach us to realize the brevity of life,
so that we may grow in wisdom.
PSALM 90:12

Think about the "lasts" that could happen today.

What if today were the last day of winter?

Or summer?

What if today were the last time your child crawled up on your lap to snuggle?

What if today were the last time you heard the voice of someone you love?

How does this change your perspective on life?

On today?

Make a list of three or four potential "lasts" that might happen to you soon.

How does this make you want to slow down and cherish the things you just wrote about before they end?

Relaxed

♥

Because so many people were coming and going that
they did not even have a chance to eat, [Jesus] said to them,
"Come with me by yourselves to a quiet place and get some rest."

MARK 6:31, NIV

Theologian Dallas Willard was asked to describe Jesus using one word. He chose *relaxed*.[2]

How might God be calling you to relax?

Perhaps by releasing control over a situation.

Or maybe by choosing not to stress over things that don't really matter.

Maybe by slowing down in order to connect with someone you typically would have missed due to your rushed lifestyle.

Whatever it is, write it down so you will remember.

- How did you do with slowing down this week?
- Which one exercise most helped you slow down and experience God in the moment?

WEEK 3

Know You Are Loved

Each day the LORD pours his unfailing love upon me.
PSALM 42:8

Do you believe, *really* believe, that God loves you? His love is not meant for you only to know about—it is meant for you to experience personally. Meditating on and receiving God's love is the foundation for how you live, make decisions, and relate to others. If you go through life with confidence that you are loved by God, you can remain secure and joyful—even when circumstances are against you.

As you meditate on and interact with the Scriptures about God's love for you, be honest with Him about your feelings. You may experience numbness, apathy, or resistance. Don't try to force yourself to feel God's love this week. God might be making you aware of a resistance to receiving His love.

Remember, it takes a lifetime to really accept and experience God's one-of-a-kind love for you. This week will simply develop an awareness of *how* you experience God's love and will give you tools for opening yourself to more of His love in the future.

I Love You This Much

♥

> This is how God loved the world: He gave His
> one and only Son, so that everyone who believes
> in Him will not perish but have eternal life.
> JOHN 3:16

How easy is it for you to believe that God loves you personally?

"God loves each of us as if there were only one of us" is a quote often attributed to Augustine, one of the great church fathers.

This week, look for ways in which God might be showing His unique love for you.

Maybe it is through a sunset, an unexpected gift, or a moment where you feel His presence.

Set a reminder on your phone or on a notepad by your bedside to end each day this week by asking yourself, "Where did I notice God's love for me today?"

Another Word for Love

♥

The Lord is compassionate and merciful, slow to get angry and filled
with unfailing love. He will not constantly accuse us, nor remain
angry forever. He does not punish us for all our sins; He does not deal
harshly with us, as we deserve. For His unfailing love toward those
who fear Him is as great as the height of the heavens above the earth.

PSALM 103:8-11

Read the above passage again, slowly.

What word or phrase stands out to you?

Make a mental note to come back to that word or phrase later
today. This is a great approach for interacting with the Scriptures
in a new way.

Ask God to reveal more this week about how this word or
phrase relates to His unique love for you.

Hindrances

♥

Can anything ever separate us from Christ's love? Does it mean He no
longer loves us if we have trouble or calamity, or are persecuted, or hungry,
or destitute, or in danger, or threatened with death? … No, despite all
these things, overwhelming victory is ours through Christ, who loved us.

ROMANS 8:35–37

Sometimes it is hard to accept another person's love. There are all
kinds of reasons for this.

Perhaps you have been hurt and fear another rejection.

Or maybe it is difficult for you to believe that someone could
actually love the real you. Sometimes it is even more difficult to
accept God's love.

What hinders you from receiving His love?

Tragedy? Shame? Doubt? Busyness? Indifference?

Think about these hindrances and talk to God about each one.

Totally and Unconditionally

I am convinced that nothing can ever separate us from God's love.
Neither death nor life, neither angels nor demons, neither our fears for
today nor our worries about tomorrow—not even the powers of hell can
separate us from God's love … that is revealed in Christ Jesus our Lord.

ROMANS 8:38–39

Allow today's Scripture to sink in. How would your life be different if you believed God loved you totally and unconditionally?

Think of someone close to you—a spouse, child, parent, or friend. Unconditionally love that person today.

Refuse to harbor bad thoughts about them. Actively encourage and bless them without expecting anything in return, assume the best of them, and gift them with an act of kindness.

You may not do this perfectly, but if you fail, thank God that He *doesn't* fail in His unconditional love for you.

A Father's Love

♥

[Jesus said,] "Let the children come to Me. Don't stop them!
For the Kingdom of God belongs to those who are like these children."
LUKE 18:16

See how very much our Father loves us,
for He calls us His children, and that is what we are!
1 JOHN 3:1

Close your eyes and imagine yourself as a child. Picture God as your Father sitting in a chair and inviting you to come sit on His lap and talk to Him about your day.

What emotions come up as you picture this scene? Do you feel uncomfortable? Nervous? Afraid? Excited? Comforted?

Share these feelings with the Lord in prayer. Ask Him to show you how these feelings impact your ability to receive His love.

Accept the Gift

May you have the power to understand, as all God's people should,
how wide, how long, how high, and how deep His love is.
May you experience the love of Christ, though it is too great
to understand fully. Then you will be made complete with
all the fullness of life and power that comes from God.
EPHESIANS 3:18-19

What gifts has God given you that you feel unworthy to receive?

Salvation? Forgiveness? Mercy? Children? Abundant resources? Special abilities or talents? How does it feel to accept
that God has given you these gifts just because He loves you?

Over the past week, when did you experience God's unique
love for you?

How did those times affect the way you interacted with others
and how you thought about yourself as a child fully loved by God?

WEEK 4

JAN. 22

Your Deepest Longing

♥

God showed His great love for us by sending
Christ to die for us while we were still sinners.

ROMANS 5:8

Everyone longs for acceptance from others. But what do we do when we feel rejected, lonely, or disappointed?

The longing for acceptance can be satisfied only when we know beyond a shadow of a doubt that we are fully accepted by the One who created us out of love.

God's love is not dependent on your behavior. He doesn't accept you less when you sin, nor does your good behavior make Him accept you more. God accepts you and loves you just as you are.

The practices this week require honesty about where you search for acceptance and how you receive God's acceptance. Let His promises of love and approval sink into your heart so that you can bravely face difficult truths about yourself without feeling condemnation.

No Doubt about It

♥

Since we have been made right in God's sight by faith,
we have peace with God because of what Jesus Christ our Lord
has done for us. Because of our faith, Christ has brought us
into this place of undeserved privilege where we now stand,
and we confidently and joyfully look forward to sharing God's glory.

ROMANS 5:1-2

Take a moment to slowly read over and meditate on God's truth from Romans 8:1: "There is no condemnation for those who belong to Christ Jesus."

When you are finished, ask yourself, *In what ways does Satan currently tempt me to doubt that God accepts me unconditionally? That God sees me as worthy and valuable? That God has a special purpose for me?*

JAN. 24

Fully Accepted

♥

[You] … were once far away from God. You were His enemies,
separated from Him by your evil thoughts and actions. Yet now He has
reconciled you to Himself through the death of Christ in His physical body.
As a result, He has brought you into His own presence, and you are
holy and blameless as you stand before Him without a single fault.

COLOSSIANS 1:21–22

What thoughts or actions, in the past or present, have hindered
you from receiving God's full acceptance?

Have you looked elsewhere for acceptance?

Have you believed you were unworthy or unholy because of
something you have done?

Have you listened to condemning thoughts?

Consider these hindrances and spend time talking to God
about each one.

No Fault

♥

Even before He made the world, God loved us and chose us in Christ
to be holy and without fault in His eyes. God decided in advance to
adopt us into His own family by bringing us to Himself through Jesus
Christ. This is what He wanted to do, and it gave Him great pleasure.

EPHESIANS 1:4–5

Imagine God thinking about you.

What do you assume God feels about you right now?

Read the verse above and reflect on how your thoughts are
similar to or different from what the Bible says God thinks of you.

Perfection Not Required

❤

Before the Passover celebration, Jesus knew that His hour had come to leave
this world and return to His Father. He had loved His disciples during His
ministry on earth, and now He loved them to the very end.

JOHN 13:1

Jesus saw His disciples at their best—and their very worst.

They argued about who was the greatest, doubted Him even
after witnessing His miracles, and betrayed Him in His time of
greatest need. Yet He still loved them.

Read the passage again. Do you believe that God's acceptance is
dependent on your being at your best?

Talk to God about where you are not perfect.

Do you gossip?

Are you easily angered?

Do you struggle with fear or pride?

Whatever challenges you, thank God for His grace and for
loving you no less because of your struggles.

For Better or for Worse

♥

God is so rich in mercy, and He loved us so much, that even though
we were dead because of our sins, He gave us life when he raised
Christ from the dead. (It is only by God's grace that you have been saved!)

EPHESIANS 2:4-5

Think back to a time when you did something you were not proud of.

Maybe you said something that hurt someone deeply, lied to make yourself look good, or perhaps even committed a crime.

Now read the verses above one more time and internalize the truth that God loves you even in your worst moments.

Tell God how this reality makes you feel.

How might this knowledge encourage you today to respond to someone who may not deserve your acceptance?

You Are Mine

♥

The One who formed you says, "Do not be afraid, for I have ransomed you. I have called you by name; you are Mine. When you go through deep waters, I will be with you. When you go through rivers of difficulty, you will not drown. When you walk through the fire of oppression ... the flames will not consume you."

ISAIAH 43:1-2

Read the passage again and imagine God is speaking directly to you. Then meditate on these statements of God's love for you:

I have rescued you. I have called you. You are Mine. I will be with you. You will not drown. You will not be consumed by oppression.

Which of these statements means the most to you? Over the past week, when have you most felt accepted by God? How might this impact your interactions with yourself and others?

WEEK 5

JAN. 29

When God Comes to Mind

♥

This is the way to have eternal life—to know You, the only
true God, and Jesus Christ, the One You sent to earth.
JOHN 17:3

What do you *really* think about God? What do you *absolutely know*
to be true about Him? Your answers to these questions impact
everything you do. "What comes into our minds when we think
about God is the most important thing about us," wrote A. W.
Tozer. [3]

Each day this week will focus on one of God's attributes. God's
"attributes" are simply who He really is and what He does. As you
read the reflection questions, be honest with yourself and God
about any inconsistencies between what you thought you knew
about God and what the Bible actually says about Him.

Resist the urge to immediately "fix" your relationship with
God in those areas where you were wrong about Him. Allow the
Holy Spirit to do the mending. Reread the Scriptures from the last
two weeks if any feelings of condemnation or shame arise. The
focus of this week is simply knowing God better.

Ever Present

---♥---

"Am I a God who is only close at hand?" says the LORD. "No, I am far away at the same time. Can anyone hide from Me in a secret place? Am I not everywhere in all the heavens and earth?" says the LORD.
JEREMIAH 23:23–24

God is not restricted by space or time. His presence fills every single atom and will continue to do so throughout eternity.

With this truth in mind, we can walk through our days with courage and confidence because our faithful God has promised always to be with us.

Knowing this reality, ask yourself these questions:

Do I believe that God is everywhere—especially that He is always with me? When was the last time I truly experienced God's presence? How might today look different if I absolutely believe God is with me?

Forgiving

♥

No matter how deep the stain of your sins, I can take
it out and make you as clean as freshly fallen snow.
ISAIAH 1:18, TLB

[You] were once far away from God.... Yet now He has reconciled
you to Himself through the death of Christ.... As a result,
He has brought you into His own presence, and you are holy
and blameless as you stand before Him without a single fault.
COLOSSIANS 1:21-22

God promises that when we ask, He forgives *all* our sins and never thinks of them again.

Feelings of shame, self-condemnation, and disgrace have no place in those who have accepted God's forgiveness.

Ask yourself, *Do I believe that God can forgive even my worst sins? When have I experienced God's forgiveness? How might today look different if I fully accept God's forgiveness?*

Faithful

♥

The LORD your God is indeed God. He is the faithful God who keeps His covenant for a thousand generations and lavishes His unfailing love on those who love Him and obey His commands.

DEUTERONOMY 7:9

God has given both His promise and His oath. These two things are unchangeable because it is impossible for God to lie. Therefore, we who have fled to Him for refuge can have great confidence as we hold to the hope that lies before us.

HEBREWS 6:18

God cannot lie, and therefore cannot break His promises. This means you never have to worry that God will change His mind about loving you unconditionally.

Knowing this truth, ask yourself, *Do I believe God is faithful to keep His promises? When have I experienced or witnessed God's faithfulness? How might today look different if I were confident in God's promises to be faithful to me?*

Good

Surely Your goodness and unfailing love will pursue me all the
days of my life, and I will live in the house of the Lord forever.

PSALM 23:6

How great is the goodness You have stored up for those
who fear You ... blessing them before the watching world.

PSALM 31:19

Taste and see that the Lord is good.
Oh, the joys of those who take refuge in Him!

PSALM 34:8

Our God is inherently good. Not only is He the perfect example of
goodness, but He also wants good things for your life. With that
truth in mind, consider these questions: *Do I believe that God is
absolutely good? When have I experienced God's goodness in my life?
How might today look different if I believe that God, who is absolutely
good, right now desires good things for me?*

Powerful

♥

He counts the stars and calls them all by name. How great is our Lord!
His power is absolute! His understanding is beyond comprehension!
PSALM 147:4–5

God is working in you, giving you the desire and the
power to do what pleases Him.... The Spirit who lives in
you is greater than the spirit who lives in the world.
PHILIPPIANS 2:13; 1 JOHN 4:4

God spoke the universe into existence, and His great power is displayed throughout His Word. This means that we can pray boldly and with great expectations, because nothing is too hard for our God.

With this reality in mind, ask yourself, *Do I believe God has ultimate power over everything? When have I experienced or seen God's power in my life? How might my prayers and attitude look different if I really believe in God's great and unlimited power?*

Trustworthy

♥

Trust in the LORD with all your heart; do not depend
on your own understanding. Seek His will in all
you do, and He will show you which path to take.

PROVERBS 3:5-6

"I know the plans I have for you," says the LORD. "They are plans
for good and not for disaster, to give you a future and a hope."

JEREMIAH 29:11

This week we have meditated on how God is present, forgiving, faithful, good, and powerful. Knowing these attributes, we can trust that He loves us and knows what is best for us. He can be trusted with the details of our days as well as the major plans for our future.

- Do you believe God has good plans for your life?
- When have you experienced God as trustworthy?
- How might today look different if you trust that God has a great plan for you?

WEEK 6

FEB. 5

Getting to Know the Real You

♦

Examine yourselves to see if your faith is genuine. Test yourselves.

2 CORINTHIANS 13:5

Theologian John Calvin stated that true wisdom consists of two things: knowledge of God and knowledge of self.[4] If we know a lot about ourselves but not about God, we become self-absorbed. If we know a lot about God but not much about ourselves, we become proud. Knowing God and knowing ourselves are both vitally important.

This week's exercises will help you get to know yourself better. Growing in awareness of the self is called "self-examination," which involves voluntarily testing and examining your heart. It is about inviting the Holy Spirit to reveal what is true about you so that you can better understand where you are in relation to God and others. The goal of this week is not to bring shame upon yourself but to bring authenticity to your life with God and others.

This week focuses on truth and creating a desire to change, and next week will focus on confession, which is how you respond when you acknowledge your true self.

Open Heart Surgery

Search me, O God, and know my heart; test me and
know my anxious thoughts. Point out anything in me that
offends You, and lead me along the path of everlasting life.

PSALM 139:23-24

Throw off your old sinful nature and your former way of life,
which is corrupted by lust and deception. Instead,
let the Spirit renew your thoughts and attitudes.

EPHESIANS 4:22-23

Picture God looking deeply into your heart and seeing all the sins within it that have the power to damage your relationship with Him and others. Then picture Him lovingly bringing those things to the surface.

As you imagine this, does any sin immediately come to mind? Before you can throw off your sin, you need to know what it is. So end this time of prayer by thanking God for helping you discover these truths about yourself.

What's in Your Heart?

Let us test and examine our ways. Let us turn back to the Lord.
LAMENTATIONS 3:40

"You must love the Lord your God with all your heart, all your soul,
all your mind, and all your strength." ... "Love your neighbor
as yourself." No other commandment is greater than these.
MARK 12:30-31

This week, consider the thoughts that enter your mind when you wake up in the morning and when you lie down at the end of the day.

Your first and last thoughts are good indicators of what is most important to you. They help reveal what you really care about—the true loves of your heart.

Over the course of the week, ask yourself whether those thoughts are focused more on your desires or on God's desires for you.

Honest Feedback

—— ♥ ——

The human heart is the most deceitful of all things,
and desperately wicked. Who really knows how bad it is?
JEREMIAH 17:9

This week, ask a close friend or family member to give you honest feedback about your weaknesses. Here are some questions to consider asking that person:

- Have I recently hurt your feelings in some way?
- Do you feel like I am present with you when we are together?
- Do you feel as though I genuinely care about your interests, dreams, or passions?
- Is there a blind spot in my life I need to become aware of?
- In what ways can I change my words and actions so I can love you better?

Without defending yourself, confess these shortcomings to your loved one and ask for forgiveness.

Why Do You Doubt?

♥

Oh, how great are God's riches and wisdom and knowledge!
How impossible it is for us to understand His decisions and His ways!

ROMANS 11:33

Timothy Keller once stated, "Worry is not believing God will get it right, and bitterness is believing God got it wrong."[5]

Talk with God about the quote and Scripture verse above.

Where do you feel anxiety or bitterness in your life?

How has that experience caused you to doubt that God wants the best for you?

Choose one phrase you can say to yourself today that will help you better trust in His infinite wisdom and knowledge. For example, you may want to say something like "God wants good things for my life," "God's decisions and ways are best," or "God's wisdom is far greater than my own."

Is It Possible?

Moses raised his hand over the sea, and the LORD opened up a path through the water with a strong east wind.... So the people of Israel walked through the middle of the sea on dry ground, with walls of water on each side!
EXODUS 14:21-22

Jesus looked at them intently and said, "Humanly speaking, it is impossible. But with God everything is possible."
MATTHEW 19:26

In what area of your life do you need the kind of help that seems impossible? Maybe it's finding a job, forgiving another person, quitting an addiction, or grieving a great loss.

Spend a moment right now talking to God about why it is hard for you to have faith and trust Him in this particular area. Memorize one of the verses above to remind you that God is all-powerful and able to do the impossible.

Who Do You Want to Be?

It is the same with My word. I send it out, and it always produces fruit.
It will accomplish all I want it to, and it will prosper everywhere I send it.
ISAIAH 55:11

The Holy Spirit produces this kind of fruit in our lives: love, joy, peace,
patience, kindness, goodness, faithfulness, gentleness, and self-control.
GALATIANS 5:22-23

Think about the kind of person you want to be in ten years. Write out which "fruit" you want to be known for.

What one step can you take today to begin to become that person?

As you think back over the past week of working on self-examination, what is one thing the Holy Spirit has shown you about yourself that you didn't realize before, positive or negative?

WEEK 7

Reconnecting to God

♥

David said to God, "I have sinned greatly....
Please forgive my guilt for doing this foolish thing."
1 CHRONICLES 21:8

It is human nature to hide and cover when we have done something wrong. Adam and Eve hid in the bushes and covered themselves with leaves after they sinned in the garden of Eden. The guilt and shame of their sin placed a relational barrier between God and them.

Do you let your sin come between you and God? If sin separates you from God, confession is the bridge that reconnects you. It allows you to go back to God so that you can receive His mercy and experience His forgiveness. Confession is essential because it reminds you of your need for Jesus and the cross.

But this can happen only when you allow the Holy Spirit to bring the darkest places of your heart into the light. As you practice confession this week, remind yourself of God's unconditional love and acceptance despite your sinful nature.

Sin Investigation

Tell me, what have I done wrong?
Show me my rebellion and my sin.
JOB 13:23

With the above verse in mind, ask yourself how often you say those words in prayer. If you were to be honest, how much importance do you place on confession?

Many people think they're pretty good, so they don't actively search the darkest corners of their hearts for sin. But when the roots of sin are left unchecked, they grow wild and untamed. Therefore it's actually healthy to root out anything in you that prevents you from having full and vibrant fellowship with God.

So pause right now and let the Holy Spirit point out something deep within you that you need to confess. Pray, "Lord, here I am. I present myself to You. I open my heart to You. Show me where I have sinned."

Hiding

♥

*When I refused to confess my sin, my body
wasted away, and I groaned all day long....
Finally, I confessed all my sins to You and
stopped trying to hide my guilt. I said to myself,
"I will confess my rebellion to the Lord."
And You forgave me! All my guilt is gone.*

PSALM 32:3, 5

Is there something you have been hiding from God and others?
What keeps you from confessing?

Fear?

Shame?

Apathy?

Denial?

Talk with God about it, remembering that He loves you and
wants to forgive you. Pray this: "Lord, I desire to please You with
every part of my day, although I know my actions don't always
show this. Show me where I hide and cover my sin so that I can
begin to allow You to love me in those dark places."

Heart Check

♥

If we claim we have no sin, we are only fooling ourselves and not
living in the truth. But if we confess our sins to Him, He is faithful
and just to forgive us our sins and to cleanse us from all wickedness.

1 JOHN 1:8-9

Spend a few minutes thinking back over your interactions with
others this week.

When did you hurt someone, either intentionally or uninten-
tionally?

When did you manipulate someone with your words or
actions?

Did you dismiss someone's feelings?

Did you neglect an apparent need?

Confess these things to God and accept His forgiveness. Pray,
"Search me, O God, and know my heart. Show me why I chose to
hurt this person. Open my heart to Your truth, so I don't deceive
myself."

Unsettled

♥

Oh, what joy for those whose disobedience is forgiven, whose sin is
put out of sight! Yes, what joy for those whose record the Lord
has cleared of guilt, whose lives are lived in complete honesty!
PSALM 32:1-2

In *God's Outrageous Claims*, apologist Lee Strobel wrote, "Few
things accelerate the peace process as much as humbly admitting
our own wrongdoing and asking forgiveness."[6]

With this quote in mind, ask yourself, *Are there areas in my life
where I don't have peace? Where I feel unsettled?* (Areas could include
a relationship, home life, work decisions, or free-time choices.)

Ask God to point out any unconfessed sin you have in these
areas. Pray, "Lord, I desire to live in complete honesty. I long to
be free from my guilt. Please show me whatever is keeping me
from experiencing joy, peace, and a full relationship with You and
with others."

Filled Up

♥

True godliness with contentment is itself great wealth.
After all, we brought nothing with us when we came into the
world, and we can't take anything with us when we leave it.
So if we have enough food and clothing, let us be content.

1 TIMOTHY 6:6-8

Can you be content with what God has given you?

Think about one thing you often wish for but don't really need and possibly may never achieve (such as a new car, a remodeled kitchen, or thicker hair).

Spend a few minutes talking to God about the places in your heart that are unsatisfied and ungrateful. Pray, "Lord, I want to experience true contentment. I confess my desire to always have more. May I be content in that for today, I have enough."

Heart Health

♥

Guard your heart above all else, for it determines the course of your life.
PROVERBS 4:23

What are you letting into your heart these days that will likely lead to a rift in your relationship with God?

Are you watching a television show or movie that isn't edifying? Listening to a radio talk show that uses crude language? Looking at websites or magazines that glorify looks, wealth, or sex? What is the first thing that comes to mind?

Spend a few minutes talking to God about this.

Now reflect over the last two weeks and answer the following questions: What have you learned about yourself (self-examination)? How has this discovery changed your communication with God (confession)?

Ask God if there is a particular sin in your life that He wants you to confess now to Him and possibly to a close, trusted friend. And then confess it.

WEEK 8

The Only Way to Grow

❤

Anyone who becomes as humble as this little child
is the greatest in the Kingdom of Heaven.

MATTHEW 18:4

Pride, at its core, is the desire to live apart from God. Pride is convincing ourselves that, on any particular issue, we know better than He does. Practicing humility is essential because it helps us confront our pride long before we reach disaster. Humility begins with knowing who God is and who we are in comparison. It is not about seeing ourselves as less, but about seeing God as so much more—as the One who is perfect in goodness and all-loving toward His creation.

This perspective helps us trust that God's plans are far better than our own. We cannot force ourselves to be humble. However, we can ask the Holy Spirit to show us where we are controlled by pride (for example, in characteristics like stubbornness, distrust that God's Word is true, hypocrisy, or arrogance). In fact, almost every sinful action stems from pride, which is why it's so important to practice humility. Without humility, we become unteachable and miss out on learning from and growing with God.

Can You Let It Go?

♥

I know, LORD, that our lives are not our own.
We are not able to plan our own course.
So correct me, LORD, but please be gentle.
JEREMIAH 10:23-24

In *The Great Divorce*, author and theologian C. S. Lewis wrote, "There are only two kinds of people in the end: those who say to God, 'Thy will be done,' and those to whom God says, in the end, '*Thy* will be done.'"[7]

Which kind of person are you?

Do you willingly submit to God's will or feel reluctance about His changes in your plans?

Think about your to-do list for today. In which area is it difficult to say to God, "Thy will be done"?

With this in mind, read the verse above as a prayer.

Your Seat at the Table

♥

When you are invited to a wedding feast, don't sit in the seat of honor ... take the lowest place at the foot of the table. Then when your host sees you, he will come and say, "Friend, we have a better place for you!" Then you will be honored in front of all the other guests.
LUKE 14:8, 10

Spend a few moments thinking about what motivates your decision of where to sit at the table (either at home or on group outings).

Do you tend to sit near those with high status, or by those with whom you are most comfortable?

Do you choose the seat with the best view?

The next time you sit around a table with a group, ask the Lord to help you choose a humble seat.

Will You Ask?

♥

Fools think their own way is right, but the wise listen to others.
PROVERBS 12:15

Get all the advice and instruction you can,
so you will be wise the rest of your life.
PROVERBS 19:20

In what area in your life would it be wise to get advice?

Maybe about a conflict in a relationship?

A financial decision?

A job change at work?

A dry time in your faith?

Help with a persistent temptation?

It takes humility to seek advice, especially in areas that are sensitive or those where people expect us to have the answers.

Think of a person who can help you with the advice you need. Exercise humility and ask them today.

O God, Have Mercy

♥

Two men went to the Temple to pray. One was a Pharisee, and the other
was a despised tax collector. The Pharisee ... prayed this prayer:
"I thank you, God, that I am not like other people—cheaters, sinners,
adulterers." ... But the tax collector ... dared not even lift his eyes to
heaven as he prayed. Instead, he beat his chest in sorrow, saying, "O God,
be merciful to me, for I am a sinner." I tell you, this sinner, not the
Pharisee, returned home justified before God. For those who exalt themselves will be humbled, and those who humble themselves will be exalted.

LUKE 18:10-14

Practice humility today by praying the words of the tax collector:
"O God, be merciful to me, for I am a sinner." Repeat this prayer
several times throughout the day.

What You're Proud Of

♥

This is what the LORD says: "Don't let the wise boast in their wisdom, or the powerful boast in their power, or the rich boast in their riches. But those who wish to boast should boast in this alone: that they truly know Me and understand that I am the LORD who demonstrates unfailing love and who brings justice and righteousness to the earth, and that I delight in these things."

JEREMIAH 9:23-24

If you were to boast about anything that you've accomplished, what would it be?

Your appearance?

Your educational degrees?

Your children's achievements?

Your latest job promotion?

Your role in your church or community?

Be honest and vulnerable with God here. Take a few minutes to think about what this passage calls believers to boast in. When was the last time you "boasted" about God's love, justice, or righteousness?

The Greatness of a Humble Future

♥

"My thoughts are nothing like your thoughts," says the LORD.
"And My ways are far beyond anything you could imagine.
For just as the heavens are higher than the earth, so My ways are
higher than your ways and My thoughts higher than your thoughts."
ISAIAH 55:8-9

Make a list of some things you are planning for your future—such as buying a home, having children, enjoying retirement, or seeking a career change.

Read over the verses above one more time with your plans in mind. Ask God what He thinks about your list.

If He shows you something to delete, are you humble enough to let it go?

If He shows you something to add to your list, can you accept it?

As you think back on this week focused on humility, what verse, question, or thought stood out to you?

WEEK 9

FEB. 26

Getting Unstuck

Teach me Your ways, O LORD, that I may live according to Your truth!

PSALM 86:11

The older we get, the more we tend to become stuck in our ways and avoid the humbling feeling of learning something new. Scripture, however, calls us to be lifelong learners, with the Lord as our primary teacher and guide.

Practicing "teachability" means being open to new ways of doing things, putting aside the need to appear intelligent or self-sufficient—being okay with not knowing it all. Life is an adventure, and God always has something new for us to learn. What if we woke up every day ready to grow with God and absorb His wisdom? Isaiah 30:20 says that even in days of pain and adversity, God wants to teach us. He longs for us to be open to learning from Him.

As you practice "teachability" this week, ask God to help you learn how to live as an eager apprentice—ready to absorb something new each day. Embrace the role of a student this week, remembering that someday, "you will see your teacher with your own eyes" (Isaiah 30:20).

Open to Learn

♥

Wisdom will enter your heart,
and knowledge will fill you with joy.
PROVERBS 2:10

Intelligent people are always ready to learn.
Their ears are open for knowledge.
PROVERBS 18:15

This week, choose to learn something new in which you have no previous experience or skill. For example, try gardening, drawing, cooking, or identifying the trees in your front yard.

Obviously you can't learn much in just a week, but you can at least gain a broad overview. You don't have to continue after this week unless you want to.

The point of this exercise is to begin disciplining yourself to be teachable. Talk to the Lord about how humbling it is to learn something you know nothing about.

Self Improvement

♥

Cry out for insight, and ask for understanding. Search for
them as you would for silver.... Then you will understand what
it means to fear the Lord.... Then you will understand what
is right, just, and fair, and you will find the right way to go.

PROVERBS 2:3-5, 9

Understand this, my dear brothers and sisters: You must all
be quick to listen, slow to speak, and slow to get angry.

JAMES 1:19

Ask someone today, "What can I do to be a better _____?"
(Fill in the blank: spouse, parent, boss, sibling, friend, neighbor,
coworker.)

Before you ask, though, take time to reread the Scripture
above to gain wisdom about how to approach this conversation.

Listen

♥

They hated knowledge and chose not to fear the LORD. They
rejected my advice and paid no attention when I corrected them.
Therefore, they must eat the bitter fruit of living their own way.

PROVERBS 1:29-31

Fools think their own way is right,
but the wise listen to others.

PROVERBS 12:15

How do you usually respond when someone corrects you or offers
constructive criticism?

Do you become irritable and defensive, or open and willing
to consider it?

The next time you are corrected, ask yourself if the constructive
criticism might actually be from God, who has prompted a person
to speak to you.

If you knew the correction was from God, would you be more
open to learning from it?

Teach Me

♥

Fools have no interest in understanding;
they only want to air their own opinions.
PROVERBS 18:2

Wise people treasure knowledge,
but the babbling of a fool invites disaster.
PROVERBS 10:14

On a scale of one to ten (one being "very open" and ten being "not open at all"), how would you rate your openness to learning new ways of doing things?

This week, ask someone to teach you *their* way of doing something. It may be as simple as cutting an onion, making a bed, budgeting, or staying organized.

Do your best to set aside your own opinions and knowledge in order to learn from someone else.

Who Can Teach Me?

—— ♥ ——

I thought, "Those who are older should speak, for wisdom comes
with age." But there is a spirit within people, the breath of the
Almighty within them, that makes them intelligent. Sometimes
the elders are not wise. Sometimes the aged do not understand justice.
JOB 32:7-9

A spiritual gift is given to each of us so we can help each other.
To one person the Spirit gives the ability to give wise advice.
1 CORINTHIANS 12:7-8

Picture yourself in ten, twenty, or thirty years. Consider three
character traits that you would like to have then. Whom do you
know with these traits who could help you become that kind of
person?

If no names come to mind, make it part of your daily prayer
to ask God to send people into your life who can teach you these
character traits.

Reflect and Learn

♥

Instruct the wise, and they will be even wiser.
Teach the righteous, and they will learn even more.

PROVERBS 9:9

Which practice in this devotional so far have you felt you needed least? How about the most?

For the practice you chose as "least needed," consider how this may reveal stubbornness to change.

For the one you chose as "most needed," thank the Lord for helping you realize a need for change in your life.

As you reflect on the past week, make note of the areas where you have grown in your desire to be more teachable. Continue to focus on those.

WEEK 10

MAR. 5

In Tune, In Touch

❤

Let those with discernment listen carefully. The paths of the Lord
are true and right, and righteous people live by walking in them.
HOSEA 14:9

Discernment is about becoming more and more sensitive to God's voice and direction. God promises that He will guide and counsel you (Psalm 32:8), lead you to truth (John 16:13), and help you listen for His voice (John 10:27). However, this happens only when you live connected to Him. Practically, this involves praying, reading Scripture, listening to God, opening yourself to His direction and to interruptions to your schedule, and recognizing how your desires and motives hinder your ability to hear Him well. Discernment is being so in tune with God's voice that you recognize it when He speaks to you.

Some of this week's exercises will ask you to involve God in decisions that may seem silly or insignificant. Remember that God desires you to invite Him into all your plans and decisions— both the big and the small. Learning to discern God's leading in small things will prepare you to better recognize His voice when the big decisions come along.

Can You Recognize My Voice?

♥

My child, listen to what I say.... Tune your ears to wisdom....
[A]sk for understanding.... [A]nd you will gain knowledge of God.
PROVERBS 2:1-3, 5

You must test them to see if the spirit they have comes from God.
1 JOHN 4:1

What tactics does Satan use to take your thoughts and intentions from God? Does he tempt you with a desire for more money or possessions? A deep need for approval from others? An excessive focus on your appearance?

As you practice discernment, ask God to help you distinguish His voice from your own, from others', and from Satan's. As you make decisions, get in the habit of pausing to question which voice is speaking to you. You can begin by asking yourself, *Is this decision leading me toward or away from God?*

Lord, Where Should I Walk?

♥

Your own ears will hear Him. Right behind you a voice will say,
"This is the way you should go," whether to the right or to the left.
ISAIAH 30:21

"The only answer to the question, how do we know whether this is from God? is *by experience*,"[8] says Dallas Willard in his book *Hearing God*.

Experience making decisions with God in a small way today. Go for a walk in your neighborhood or in a park.

As you walk, continually ask God, "Where would you like me to go? To the left or to the right?"

This may feel like guesswork, but trust that this is a small step to begin asking God questions and listening for His answers.

Notice the people or places that cross your path. God may invite you to make conversation with someone or simply sit alone in a beautiful place.

What Really Matters?

♥

I pray that your love will overflow more and more, and that
you will keep on growing in knowledge and understanding.
For I want you to understand what really matters, so that you may
live pure and blameless lives until the day of Christ's return.

PHILIPPIANS 1:9-10

Think over the items on your agenda today. Practice being open to
God's will as you ask Him to help you discern what really matters.

Then reflect on the following questions:

· What really *needs* to get done today?
· What on my schedule can I let go of today?
· Is there something that is not on my agenda today that the Lord
may be asking me to add?

Listen ... and Speak

♥

That night Paul had a vision: A man from Macedonia in northern Greece was standing there, pleading with him, "Come over to Macedonia and help us!" So we decided to leave for Macedonia at once, having concluded that God was calling us to preach the Good News there.
ACTS 16:9-10

Ask the Lord whom He might be leading you to connect with today.

Is there an old friend or family member you haven't spoken to in a long time who comes to mind?

Send that person a thoughtful text or a card, or call and let them know the Lord put them on your heart.

Lead Me, Lord

♥

The LORD says, "I will guide you along the best pathway
for your life. I will advise you and watch over you."
PSALM 32:8

You probably drive the same route regularly to get to certain places. But when you get in your car today, ask the Lord which route He would like you to take. Be open to how God might lead you in a different way.

There is no wrong way to do this exercise. This is about learning to ask and then listening to the voice of the Lord so you can be more discerning as He leads you in other ways.

Is It Time to Wait?

♥

Wait patiently for the LORD.... Yes, wait patiently for the LORD.
PSALM 27:14

Be still in the presence of the LORD, and wait patiently for Him to act.
PSALM 37:7

When we are tired, overworked, overwhelmed, or disconnected from God, it is wise to put off making big decisions until we are in a healthier place.

Think about a decision that you need to make.

Are you considering a job change?

How to spend your money?

Whether or not to have a difficult conversation?

Now reflect on your present circumstances and ask the Lord if this is the best time to make that decision.

As you end this week on discernment, look back through the last six days and ask the Lord if there is an exercise He would like you to repeat.

WEEK 11

MAR. 12

From Tears to Celebration

❤

Let all who take refuge in You rejoice; let them sing
joyful praises forever. Spread Your protection over them,
that all who love Your name may be filled with joy.

PSALM 5:11

Satan's mission is to kill, steal, and destroy everything good in your life—especially your joy. So how can you remain joyful in a world where there is so much to be sad about?

God's Word says that joy is good medicine for the heart and the source of our strength, transforming our tearful moments into times of celebration. Being joyful means choosing an attitude of appreciation, thanksgiving, and rejoicing.

The exercises this week will help you learn to appreciate the gifts God has given you, develop an attitude of thanksgiving, and rejoice with God in response. Remember that it is impossible to force yourself to feel joy. But you can ask the Lord to help you be aware of His gifts and goodness in your life, which will help you develop an appreciative and thankful heart—regardless of your circumstances.

First Thoughts for Your Day

♥

This is the day the LORD has made.
We will rejoice and be glad in it.
PSALM 118:24

Write out this Scripture and place it next to your alarm clock or on the bathroom mirror so that it's the first thing you see every morning for the next week.

Read the verse to yourself three times each day, allowing it to impact your attitude and set your focus for the rest of the day.

Then ask the Lord to help you anticipate all He has in store for you and the things He will be doing around you in the coming hours.

Good Medicine

♥

A joyful heart is good medicine,
but a crushed spirit dries up the bones.
PROVERBS 17:22, ESV

As you look ahead to this day, what is the one part of it in which you will struggle most to be joyful?

Pause and ask God to open your heart and give you a joyful perspective about it; then read the above verse again.

Sometimes joy is a reaction to a happy circumstance. Other times, you must choose to be joyful even when it feels as though you have nothing to be joyful about.

How might God be calling you to choose joy today?

God Delights in You

♥

The LORD delights in His people; He crowns the humble
with victory. Let the faithful rejoice that He honors them.
Let them sing for joy as they lie on their beds.

PSALM 149:4-5

Who in your life brings you the most joy?

Your spouse? Your child? A best friend?

If you, in your fallen and sinful condition, can rejoice over
this person, how much more does your perfect heavenly Father
rejoice over you?

Take a moment and let that sink in: The God of the universe
delights in you right now, regardless of what you've done.

How would your attitude change if you really believed God was
cheering you on throughout this day?

Smile

♥

You will show me the way of life, granting me the joy of
Your presence and the pleasures of living with You forever.
PSALM 16:11

Let all that I am praise the LORD; may I never
forget the good things He does for me.
PSALM 103:2

Think of your happiest memory. What is it about this memory
that made you feel so happy?

Reflect on that memory for a while and try to recapture the
feeling of joy you had at that moment. Let yourself smile.

Now rejoice with God for the gift of that memory and for His
promise—what you've experienced in your happiest moment is
just a taste of what you will eventually experience every day for
all eternity.

The Joy of Adversity

♥

We know that God causes everything to work together for the good of
those who love God and are called according to His purpose for them.
ROMANS 8:28

Dear brothers and sisters, when troubles of any kind
come your way, consider it an opportunity for great joy.
JAMES 1:2

What is one trial you are currently facing? How might God use this adversity as an opportunity for you to experience great joy? Is this experience making you trust Him more? Is it humbling you? Is it causing you to be grateful for the good things in your life?

This is a hard exercise because it pushes against the direction your heart wants to go, the way of discouragement, sadness, and even bitterness. Pray that God will allow joy to push back so you can experience God's promise to bring good out of difficult circumstances.

Enjoy Today!

♥

Go ahead. Eat your food with joy, and drink your
wine with a happy heart, for God approves of this!

ECCLESIASTES 9:7

How might the above verse encourage you to be more intentional about enjoying today?

Perhaps by taking your time and not rushing? Eating something special? Practicing gratitude? Going on a spontaneous adventure?

Author Ann Voskamp wrote on her blog, "Joy isn't about how much our lives have—but how much we enjoy our lives."[9]

Where could you create space in your schedule to enjoy life more today?

Over the past week, how has meditating on joy impacted your perspective, attitude, and relationship with God? Was there a moment or day when you were thankful you chose to rejoice?

WEEK 12

What Can I Say?

♥

Pray in the Spirit at all times and on every occasion.
Stay alert and be persistent in your prayers.
EPHESIANS 6:18

Have you ever been in a situation with someone where you just couldn't think of anything to say? Have you ever experienced this in your relationship with God?

As in other relationships, almost every believer goes through seasons where talking to God feels stale, one-sided, unexciting, or even frustrating. Sometimes this is the result of unconfessed sin or because we are reluctant to get personal with God about our deepest needs and desires. Other times, God remains silent as a way to strengthen our faith. Whatever the case, the apostle John offers us some much-needed encouragement: "We are confident that He hears us" (1 John 5:4).

This week focuses on specific exercises to deepen and energize your conversations with God. Prayer is not just about telling Him what your needs are—it's about engaging with the ever-present Christ in every moment. As you talk with God this week, keep in mind that you're forming and deepening the most important relationship you will ever have.

Why Do You Pray?

When you pray, don't be like the hypocrites who love to pray publicly
on street corners and in the synagogues where everyone can see them.
I tell you the truth, that is all the reward they will ever get. But when you
pray, go away by yourself, shut the door behind you, and pray to your
Father in private. Then your Father, who sees everything, will reward you.

MATTHEW 6:5–6

What motivates you to pray?

Is it that you feel like you should?

You need something from God?

You want to know Him more?

You desire to be a better person?

Don't be afraid to have an honest conversation with God about
why you pray. Ask Him to reveal your real motives for praying.

But first remind yourself that God accepts, delights in, and
unconditionally loves you.

Don't Stop Talking

Jesus told His disciples a story to show that they should always pray and never give up. "There was a judge … who neither feared God nor cared about people. A widow of that city came to him repeatedly, saying, 'Give me justice in this dispute with my enemy.' The judge ignored her for a while, but finally he said to himself, '… This woman is driving me crazy. I'm going to see that she gets justice, because she is wearing me out with her constant requests!'" Then [Jesus] said, "Learn a lesson from this unjust judge. Even he rendered a just decision in the end. So don't you think God will surely give justice to His chosen people who cry out to Him day and night?"

LUKE 18:1-7

With this parable in mind, talk to God about a specific prayer request.

Talk about Anything

Peter said to Jesus, "Explain to us ..."
MATTHEW 15:15

Don't worry about anything; instead, pray about everything.
Tell God what you need, and thank Him for all He has done.
PHILIPPIANS 4:6

Learn to bring everything into your prayer life—even your distractions. Sit quietly in the presence of the Lord for a minute or so.

If distractions come to mind, talk to God about those. Remember, you are learning to talk with God, so talk to Him about anything, even if it seems trivial or you are ashamed of what you are thinking.

If you feel free to share something with your closest friend, how much more freedom should you feel to share with God, your Creator, who loves you unconditionally?

What Are You Afraid Of?

♥

David asked God, "Should I go …?"
1 CHRONICLES 14:10

O Lord, You have examined my heart and know everything about me.
PSALM 139:1

Whatever you ask in prayer, you will receive, if you have faith.
MATTHEW 21:22, ESV

Is there something you've wanted to ask God for, but you felt as if you couldn't?

What keeps you from asking?

Do you feel like you don't deserve to ask or fear God will reject your request?

Do you believe God doesn't care about your desires?

Talk to God about this and remind yourself that He already knows every desire in your heart.

A Conversation with the Almighty

❤

Pray like this: Our Father in heaven, may Your name be kept holy. May Your Kingdom come soon. May Your will be done on earth, as it is in heaven. Give us today the food we need, and forgive us our sins, as we have forgiven those who sin against us. And don't let us yield to temptation, but rescue us from the evil one.

MATTHEW 6:9–13

Read the above passage again slowly, but this time pray it to God. Remember that you are enjoying the privilege of conversing with the almighty God of the universe.

What stands out as you pray through these words?

Talk with God about why this part of the passage stands out from the rest.

As you engage in this exercise, picture yourself sitting with God and conversing about His Word.

Comfortable Conversation

♥

*If you need wisdom, ask our generous God, and He will
give it to you. He will not rebuke you for asking.*
JAMES 1:5

What is a small decision you can talk about with God today?

Whether or not to run an errand?

Which friend to call this afternoon?

What to do with your evening?

This exercise is meant to help you get in the habit of talking with God about both the big and the small decisions throughout your day.

As you think back over this week, reflect on a moment when you felt a little more comfortable talking with God.

Which exercise helped the most?

How can you incorporate that into your daily routine?

WEEK 13

MAR. 26

Soul Starved

♥

Times of refreshment will come from the presence of the Lord.
ACTS 3:20

Most of us race through life trying to meet one demand after another. This kind of treadmill existence will inevitably wear us down and starve our souls. It is impossible to effectively serve from a depleted soul. Eventually, we will pass out.

Caring for yourself means carving out enough time to care for your own soul. This is not self-centeredness; caring for yourself creates space in your heart for God and others. Even Jesus had to get away from the crowds in order to experience rest and refreshment (see Mark 6:31).

This week's exercises aim to care for your heart, mind, and body—all of which make up the soul. Since God created each person uniquely, what restores your soul may be different from what someone else needs.

As you pay attention to the practices, people, and activities that most refresh you and connect you with God, you will learn to value yourself as God values you. Give yourself permission to set aside time with God this week for the sake of your soul.

Slow Down to Fill Up

Despite Jesus' instructions, the report of His power spread even faster, and vast crowds came to hear Him preach and to be healed of their diseases. But Jesus often withdrew to the wilderness for prayer.

LUKE 5:15-16

Schedule a time this week to get away from your everyday demands and do something with the Lord to help restore your soul.

Take a long walk, read a book, enjoy a bubble bath, or visit a coffee shop. Think of this time as just resting with the Lord by inviting Him to join you during this activity.

As you end your time, ask the Lord to reveal to you what to let go of so you can have more times of soul care with Him.

Thirsty?

O God, You are my God; I earnestly search for You. My soul thirsts for You.

PSALM 63:1

If someone asked you to describe what your soul looks like, what would you say?

Is it thirsty or satisfied?

Chaotic or peaceful?

Confused or purposeful?

Fearful or confident?

Dark or light?

Weary or refreshed?

Empty or full of hope, love, and joy?

Take a moment to "check in" with God about the current state of your soul. Reflect on the word God brings to mind. Keep that word in front of you this week to remind you to care for your soul.

Soul Connections

♥

Don't you realize that your body is the temple of the Holy Spirit, Who lives in you and was given to you by God? You do not belong to yourself, for God bought you with a high price. So you must honor God with your body.
1 CORINTHIANS 6:19–20

Choose one way that you can better care for your body today. Perhaps you could cut out your favorite junk food, take the stairs, park at the far end of the lot and walk, or get to bed earlier.

Research shows that the more you care for your body, the more alert your mind is. And Scripture shows that the more alert your mind is, the more you are aware of God's work all around you.

Take a few moments to consider prayerfully how your choice to care for your body will also care for your soul.

Mind Your Soul

♥

We are God's masterpiece. He has created us anew in Christ Jesus,
so we can do the good things He planned for us long ago.
EPHESIANS 2:10

Write these two sentences on a piece of paper: (1) "I am God's masterpiece," and (2) "He has planned good things for my life."

Place this paper where you will see it throughout the day, such as on the mirror, your dashboard, the kitchen counter, or the refrigerator.

As you do this, remind yourself that you are caring for your mind and heart by focusing on truths from God's Word.

What God Really Thinks of You

♥

Thank You for making me so wonderfully complex!
Your workmanship is marvelous—how well I know it....
How precious are Your thoughts about me, O God.
They cannot be numbered!

PSALM 139:14, 17

What precious thoughts might God be thinking about you right now?

Are you funny? Creative? Good at details? A caring friend? Talented in a particular area?

Thank the Lord for creating you wonderfully unique and complex and ask Him to help you value yourself the way He values you.

Send yourself an email or text message with the words from the verse above: *How precious are Your thoughts about me, O God.*

Read it several times today, thanking God that He loves you so much.

Deep Roots, Nourished Soul

♥

They are like trees planted along a riverbank, with roots that reach deep into
the water. Such trees are not bothered by the heat or worried by long months
of drought. Their leaves stay green, and they never stop producing fruit.
JEREMIAH 17:8

Schedule a time today or tomorrow to buy a plant for your home.
As you care for this plant, allow it to be a continual reminder of
how important it is to also care for yourself.

In the past week, which activities, people, or places have refreshed your soul the most?

How might God be inviting you to make those experiences a
part of your life's regular rhythm?

WEEK 14

Why We Serve

♥

> Even the Son of Man came not to be served but to serve
> others and to give His life as a ransom for many.
>
> MATTHEW 20:28

Servants know how to set aside some of their own needs, desires, and agendas to instead seek out and meet the needs of others. Practicing service begins by being intentional in recognizing the needs around you and then meeting them.

This is an important practice because when you serve others, you are actually doing exactly what Jesus would have done—blessing someone else by meeting a deep need in their life. When you serve others, you are helping them see Jesus.

The exercises this week encourage you to pay attention to opportunities to serve. You may miss some opportunities, and that is okay. Talk to God about this and receive His grace. Remember that serving can sometimes be difficult and often requires sacrifice. If serving is hard for you, ask the Holy Spirit to show you the places in your heart where you feel resistant. Trust that He will help you serve from your heart as you serve with your body.

Searching to Serve

Jesus called them together and said, "You know that the rulers in this world lord it over their people, and officials flaunt their authority over those under them. But among you it will be different. Whoever wants to be a leader among you must be your servant, and whoever wants to be first among you must be the slave of everyone else."

MARK 10:42-44

Does serving others come naturally to you, or does it require intentionality and effort?

Ask the Lord to open your eyes and heart this week so you can see and act on opportunities to serve those around you.

Write the word *serve* on a sticky note and post it on your bathroom mirror to remind you to be on the lookout for a way to serve someone each day this week.

Six Ways to Serve Today

♥

[Jesus said,] "I was hungry, and you fed Me. I was thirsty,
and you gave Me a drink. I was a stranger, and you invited Me
into your home. I was naked, and you gave Me clothing. I was sick,
and you cared for Me. I was in prison, and you visited Me....
When you did it to one of the least of these ... you were doing it to Me!"

MATTHEW 25:35-36, 40

Reflect on the six different ways to serve from the above Scripture:

• Feed someone.
• Give someone a drink.
• Invite a lonely person into your home.
• Give someone clothing.
• Care for someone sick.
• Visit someone who is shut in.

Choose one of these six ways to serve today and imagine you are serving Jesus. How does this affect your perspective on servanthood?

The Hardest Person to Serve

Love your enemies! Do good to them. Lend to them without
expecting to be repaid. Then your reward from heaven will
be very great, and you will truly be acting as children of the
Most High, for He is kind to those who are unthankful and wicked.

LUKE 6:35

It's not hard to serve those we love, but sometimes God tests our
hearts by asking us to serve outside our comfort zones.

How might God be calling you to serve a difficult person in a
simple and unexpected way today?

Perhaps by giving a random gift, offering congratulations on a
significant accomplishment, or sending a thoughtful text?

Unwrapping Your Gift

♥

God has given each of you a gift from His great variety
of spiritual gifts. Use them well to serve one another.
1 PETER 4:10

Look up the spiritual gifts mentioned in 1 Corinthians 12:7-10 and Romans 12:6-8. In addition, go online and find a resource that provides specific definitions of the spiritual gifts.

Which spiritual gifts do you think the Lord has given you? Pray about these gifts and ask God how He would like you to use your gifts to serve others.

What steps can you take this week toward serving in these ways?

The Sacrifice of Service

♥

We know what real love is because Jesus gave up His life
for us. So we also ought to give up our lives for our
brothers and sisters.... Dear children, let's not merely say
that we love each other; let us show the truth by our actions.

1 JOHN 3:16, 18

Ask someone in your household or a close friend what you can do for them today, and then do it!

Reflect on where you recognize a resistance to serve. What is one way you can push through that resistance?

Perhaps by praying as you serve?

Imagining you are serving God?

Meditating on today's Scripture?

Remember, if you only served others when you felt like it, then you would probably never serve. Sometimes you must lead with your body and your heart will follow.

Grateful Service

♥

Be sure to fear the LORD and faithfully serve Him.
Think of all the wonderful things He has done for you.

1 SAMUEL 12:24

Is there a person or people in your life whom you find it difficult to happily serve?

Your church?

Your spouse?

A child with a bad attitude?

Your needy neighbor?

As you read the above verse again, think about some of the wonderful things God has done for you. How might this encourage you to serve with gratitude?

Think about what it has felt like to serve God by helping others this past week.

When did it seem most difficult to serve?

What exercises have best prepared your heart for service?

WEEK 15

Quieting the Noise

The LORD is in His holy Temple. Let all the earth be silent before Him.
HABAKKUK 2:20

We live in a world of noise, interruptions, and distractions where people, activities, and electronic devices are constantly vying for our attention. Because of this, many people experience silence as unfamiliar and uncomfortable.

So does silence really have a purpose? Is it even important in our relationship with God? Silence creates a space to hear from God more clearly. Practicing silence isn't only for the sake of "peace and quiet." Silence quiets the inner and outer voices in our days so that we can be alert and better listen to God.

This week, remind yourself that hearing God speak isn't the goal of silence. The goal is simply to show up and say, "God, I am listening if You have anything to say to me." And if God does decide to speak, then accept it as a gift! Lean into the discomfort of silence and learn to become more comfortable in the quiet. Each time you sit in silence with God, He is slowly teaching you to recognize His voice.

Rest in the Quiet

♥

This is what the Sovereign Lord, the Holy One of Israel, says:
"Only in returning to me and resting in Me will you
be saved. In quietness and confidence is your strength."
ISAIAH 30:15

How do you usually experience silence?

Do you long for more of it?

Does it feel lonely?

Do you try to avoid it?

Ask the Lord to help you be open to His presence. Be patient with yourself as you practice silence this week.

Start by setting a timer on your phone or clock for one minute. After you press "start," do not look at the timer again until it rings.

If you haven't done this before, a minute will seem like a long time! Close your eyes and sit in God's presence, just content to be with Him.

In Waiting, You Hear

♥

Let all that I am wait quietly before God, for my hope is in Him.
PSALM 62:5

Drive without music or the radio today to practice being with God in silence. You may need to put a sticky note on your device to remind you not to turn it on.

As you drive, talk to God if something comes to mind, but focus more on being quiet and resetting your heart to be in tune with His, listening for what He has to say to you.

This exercise is about building a habit of creating and being comfortable with silent spaces during your normal routine.

Experience the Calm

♥

Soon a fierce storm came up. High waves were breaking into the boat, and it began to fill with water. Jesus was sleeping at the back of the boat with His head on a cushion. The disciples woke Him up, shouting, "Teacher, don't You care that we're going to drown?" When Jesus woke up, He rebuked the wind and said to the waves, "Silence! Be still!" Suddenly the wind stopped, and there was a great calm.

MARK 4:37–39

Read the above passage again, but this time imagine you are on the boat with Jesus:

Listen to the waves breaking against the boat.

Feel the cold water as the boat begins to fill.

Watch Jesus awake and rebuke the storm.

What is it like to see the waves disappear and the water become still as glass?

Sit on the boat and breathe deeply. What do you feel?

Softly Spoken

— ♥ —

After the wind there was an earthquake, but the Lord was not in the
earthquake. And after the earthquake there was a fire, but the Lord was
not in the fire. And after the fire there was the sound of a gentle whisper.

1 KINGS 19:11-12

Practice being with the Lord in silence by breathing deeply and
slowly. Pay attention to the sounds around you. What do you hear?

The quiet breathing of your napping children?

Sounds of nature?

The humming of appliances in your home?

Your heartbeat?

Thank God for the opportunity to hear those things you could
have missed if you hadn't been silent.

Talking Silence

❤

The heart of the godly thinks carefully before speaking;
the mouth of the wicked overflows with evil words.
PROVERBS 15:28

In conversations with others today, practice incorporating more quiet into the conversation instead of speaking words just to fill the silence.

Be intentional about allowing space before commenting, giving advice, or asking questions.

Then set a reminder for the end of the day to check in with yourself about how you did. How can you improve in making space for silence in conversations tomorrow?

Perhaps you can count to three before speaking?

Quickly pray before responding?

Refrain from speaking during lags in the conversation?

Silent Prayer

They were trying to trap Him into saying something they could
use against Him, but Jesus stooped down and wrote in the dust
with His finger. They kept demanding an answer, so He stood up
again and said, "All right, but let the one who has never sinned throw
the first stone!" Then He stooped down again and wrote in the dust.
JOHN 8:6-8

This passage seems to suggest that Jesus remained silent long
enough for the religious leaders to keep demanding an answer
from Him.

Pause for a moment to take a difficult situation to God in
prayer, and then spend some time in silence.

After you have been silent for a few minutes, ask God if there
is anything He would like to say to you about this.

How did silence help you notice the presence and work of God
this week?

WEEK 16

Enjoy and Glorify

❤

You are worthy, O Lord our God, to receive glory
and honor and power. For You created all things,
and they exist because You created what You pleased.
REVELATION 4:11

Have you ever experienced incredible joy yet still felt like there was something missing? Maybe it was a beautiful sunset, your child's first belly laugh, or the wedding of a close friend.

C. S. Lewis wrote, "Fully to enjoy is to glorify."[10] Our joy in something is made complete when we give praise and glory to the One who gave it to us. This is worship. Dallas Willard expressed a similar sentiment: "In worship we … express the greatness, beauty, and goodness of God through thought and the use of words, rituals, and symbols."[11]

This week, release yourself from the expectation of having a divine encounter with God. Perhaps He is teaching you to worship Him for who He is and not for an experience. Some exercises will help you be honest about who or what you truly worship. Other exercises will involve reflecting on God's beauty in the world and His goodness in your life, and then responding with praise to Him.

Worship Is Thankfulness

♥

Praise the LORD! I will thank the LORD with all my heart as I meet with His godly people. How amazing are the deeds of the LORD! All who delight in Him should ponder them.

PSALM 111:1-2

Sing psalms and hymns and spiritual songs to God with thankful hearts.

COLOSSIANS 3:16

Participate in worship at your church this week or arrange a time for worship and singing at home with your family, small group, or close friends.

Think deeply about the words you are singing.

What do these songs say about who God is?

How do they lead you toward gratitude for all He has done?

Worship Is Beauty

When I look at the night sky and see the work of Your fingers
—the moon and the stars You set in place—
what are mere mortals that You should think about them,
human beings that You should care for them?

PSALM 8:3-5

The heavens proclaim the glory of God.
The skies display His craftsmanship.
Day after day they continue to speak;
night after night they make Him known.

PSALM 19:1-2

Go outside several times throughout the day and look up at the sky (preferably at sunrise, at sunset, and after dark).

Take in its vastness, variety of colors, and cloud formations, and the moon and myriad of stars.

What do you feel as you stand below this display of God's art? Allow this time to lead your heart to worship the creator of the heavens and the earth.

Worship Is Praising God with Words and Songs

I will sing to the LORD as long as I live.
I will praise my God to my last breath!
PSALM 104:33

The jailer put them into the inner dungeon and
clamped their feet in the stocks. Around midnight
Paul and Silas were praying and singing hymns
to God, and the other prisoners were listening.
ACTS 16:24–25

Paul and Silas worshiped in word and song even while in prison. Choose to praise God in an unusual place or situation this week— perhaps at the grocery store, at the gym, or in the car.

Worship by praising God for who He is, or sing or hum a favorite song about Him. When you do this, remind yourself that you are transforming a mundane moment into a time of worship.

APR. 20

Worship Is Joy

♥

Let the godly rejoice. Let them be glad in God's presence.
Let them be filled with joy.
PSALM 68:3

O LORD, I will honor and praise Your name,
for You are my God. You do such wonderful things!
You planned them long ago, and now You have accomplished them.
ISAIAH 25:1

What gives you the most joy? Your family or friends? A hobby?
Your church or ministry?

Read the verses above once more with this person or thing
in mind. Then give praise and glory to the Lord with thanks for
giving you something that brings you such joy.

Worship Is Remaining Faithful through Trials

❤

Even though the fig trees have no blossoms, and there are no grapes on the vines; even though the olive crop fails, and the fields lie empty and barren; even though the flocks die in the fields, and the cattle barns are empty, yet I will rejoice in the LORD! I will be joyful in the God of my salvation!

HABAKKUK 3:17–18

We can rejoice, too, when we run into problems and trials, for we know that they help us develop endurance. And endurance develops strength of character, and character strengthens our confident hope of salvation.

ROMANS 5:3–4

Is your worship of God dependent upon His blessings in your life? How easy or difficult has it been for you to worship God through trials? Reflect on a previous trial. What things can you worship God for as you look back?

Worship Is Reflecting on God's Faithfulness

--- ♥ ---

I love the LORD because He hears my voice and my prayer for mercy.
Because He bends down to listen, I will pray as long as I have breath!
Death wrapped its ropes around me; the terrors of the grave
overtook me. I saw only trouble and sorrow. Then I called on the
name of the LORD: "Please, LORD, save me!" How kind the LORD is!
How good He is! So merciful, this God of ours! The LORD protects
those of childlike faith; I was facing death, and He saved me.
Let my soul be at rest again, for the LORD has been good to me.

PSALM 116:1-7

Using the psalm above as a model, write a psalm of worship based
on your life.

Who has God been to you?

What qualities do you love most about Him?

What good things has He done?

WEEK 17

APR. 23

Satisfied with Love

Satisfy us each morning with Your unfailing love,
so we may sing for joy to the end of our lives.
PSALM 90:14

Contentment is one of life's most elusive qualities. Real contentment means being at peace with God and accepting how He has made you, where He has placed you, what He has given you, and who you are in relation to Him. It is trusting He has a plan for you and will accomplish it.

You grow in contentment as you trust that God is in control and is working out His unique and wonderful plan for your life. The practice of contentment results in freedom, gratitude, and joy. When you are truly content, you are free from the need to strive, spend, and compete with others because you are full of gratitude that you have more than you deserve. Contentment protects you from jealousy, covetousness, and greed.

This week, be honest with God when you feel discontent. Allow Him to use these exercises to change your heart to be at peace with who you are and who God is, and to accept that as enough for the moment.

No One like You

♥

Peter asked Jesus, "What about him, Lord?" Jesus replied, "If I want him
to remain alive until I return, what is that to you? As for you, follow Me."
JOHN 21:21-22

Pay careful attention to your own work, for then you will get the
satisfaction of a job well done, and you won't need to compare yourself
to anyone else. For we are each responsible for our own conduct.
GALATIANS 6:4-5

Where are you most tempted to compare yourself to others? Your
appearance, career, kids, or finances? The size of your home or
the number of your material possessions?

Take a few moments to confess this to God and then thank
Him for what you do have. For example, when you find yourself
wishing you looked as great as your friend, thank God for specific
features that are unique to you.

Advertisements as Reminders

Let them praise the LORD for His great love and for
the wonderful things He has done for them. For He
satisfies the thirsty and fills the hungry with good things.

PSALM 107:8–9

Everything else is worthless when compared with
the infinite value of knowing Christ Jesus my Lord.

PHILIPPIANS 3:8

When you see advertisements this week on television or billboards, online, or in your mail, use them as reminders to thank God for what you do have and for what He has given you.

This exercise will help you become habituated to pray, "Lord, You are enough" when you see an ad that communicates you are not enough until you have something more.

Is It Enough?

♥

"What should we do?" asked some soldiers. John replied, "Don't extort money or make false accusations. And be content with your pay."

LUKE 3:14

Guard against every kind of greed. Life is not measured by how much you own.... Look at the lilies and how they grow. They don't work or make their clothing, yet Solomon in all his glory was not dressed as beautifully as they are. And if God cares so wonderfully for flowers that are here today and thrown into the fire tomorrow, He will certainly care for you.

LUKE 12:15, 27–28

How content are you with your income? There is nothing wrong with wanting to earn more. The real question is: Can you be content with what you have now?

Take a few moments to pray about your answer and about how Jesus' words about money make you feel.

Relax and Receive

♥

Their voices rose in a great chorus of protest against Moses and Aaron.
"If only we had died in Egypt, or even here in the wilderness!"
they complained. "Why is the LORD taking us to this country?
... Wouldn't it be better for us to return to Egypt?"
NUMBERS 14:2-3

The Lord rescued the Israelites from slavery in Egypt, yet they still complained and struggled with discontent.

In what ways do you struggle to be content with where God has placed you?

Maybe it feels difficult to accept your season in life. Or perhaps you struggle to find contentment with your geographical location or home.

Now read Jeremiah 29:11-14.

How can these verses encourage you to be content with your current season or location in life, knowing that God has good things in store for your future?

God Doesn't Make Mistakes

♥

What are mere mortals that You should think about them,
human beings that You should care for them? Yet You made them
only a little lower than God and crowned them with glory and honor.
PSALM 8:4-5

Nothing can ever separate us from God's love.
ROMANS 8:38

The enemy often tries to make us discontent with who we are. Read the above verses again. With these words in mind, remind yourself of how God sees you—as a unique human He created, cares for, and loves deeply. He crowns you with glory and honor.

Thankfulness grows your contentment, so take time to thank God for how He made you and how much He loves you. Write these words on a piece of paper: "Lord, thank You for making me just the person You wanted me to be." Carry it with you all day, reading it often.

The Key to Confidence

---♥---

Don't love money; be satisfied with what you have.
For God has said, "I will never fail you. I will never abandon
you." So we can say with confidence, "The LORD is my helper,
so I will have no fear. What can mere people do to me?"

HEBREWS 13:5-6

Think of something you are discontent with in your life right now:

Your job or marriage?

Your appearance?

Feelings of inadequacy in a certain area?

Now read this verse again and imagine the Lord speaking these words directly to you: "(Insert your name), I will never fail you. I will never abandon you."

How do God's words to you make you feel?

Ask Him to help you feel satisfied today with what you have and confident in who you are so that you may experience a life of joy with Him.

WEEK 18

Keep Less, Give More

♥

You must each decide in your heart how much to give.
And don't give reluctantly or in response to pressure.
"For God loves a person who gives cheerfully."
2 CORINTHIANS 9:7

The world encourages us to make more and keep more. The Bible, however, focuses on how much we should give away. The way we spend our money reveals what we care most about.

Generosity doesn't just involve giving money to help others—it also concerns the giving of our time, talents, and possessions. We give because everything we have was given to us (see 1 Chronicles 29:14). Generosity is important because it teaches us to trust God with our resources and put others before ourselves. When we give, it helps us release our grip on the things we hold too tightly.

The exercises this week could be hard if God shows you a treasure in your heart that has taken priority over Him. Talk to Him about the areas where you find it hard to be generous. Ask Him to unleash the gift of generosity in you so that you can receive the joy that comes from giving.

Random Act of Giving

♥

The generous will prosper; those who
refresh others will themselves be refreshed.
PROVERBS 11:25

Remember the words of the Lord Jesus:
"It is more blessed to give than to receive."
ACTS 20:35

Look for an opportunity today to practice generosity with your finances. Ask the Lord to help you obey His promptings.

For instance, you may sense He wants you to pay for the person behind you in the drive-through, offer to fill up someone's tank at a gas station, or buy a meaningful gift for someone.

Later on, take time to reflect on how you felt just after your act of generosity.

Generous Hospitality

❤

[All the believers] met in homes for the Lord's Supper,
and shared their meals with great joy and generosity.

ACTS 2:46

Practice the generosity of hospitality like the believers in the book of Acts by inviting someone over this week for dinner or dessert.

Use this opportunity to share with them by cooking or buying a beautiful meal and enjoying warm fellowship together.

Go to your calendar right now, find an open evening, and email or text someone an invitation.

The Paradox of Giving

♥

God will generously provide all you need. Then you will always
have everything you need and plenty left over to share with others.
2 CORINTHIANS 9:8

In *The Treasure Principle*, Randy Alcorn wrote, "The more you give, the more comes back to you, because God is the greatest giver in the universe, and He won't let you outgive Him. Go ahead and try. See what happens."[12]

Do you ever fear giving too much and coming up short for yourself?

Do you sometimes think that if you give more to others, you won't have enough?

Do you worry that God's resources will run out?

Can you trust God to provide what you need?

Take a chance today: Give to someone in need so generously that it hurts, and then watch what God does in return.

Valued Treasure

Jesus told him, "If you want to be perfect, go and sell all your possessions and give the money to the poor, and you will have treasure in heaven. Then come, follow Me." But when the young man heard this, he went away sad, for he had many possessions.

MATTHEW 19:21-22

What is something you could give that would *really* be a sacrifice for you?

Perhaps a large financial gift, a possession you own that someone else admires, or your time during a busy week?

How can you begin the process of giving this gift today?

As you think about this huge act of generosity, tell the Lord how it feels to let this treasure go, and ask Him to replace it with peace and joy.

Generous Measures

♥

Give, and you will receive. Your gift will return to you in full—pressed
down, shaken together to make room for more, running over, and poured
into your lap. The amount you give will determine the amount you get back.

LUKE 6:38

How can you be generous with your time today?

Perhaps by letting someone go first in line at the grocery store
or writing that belated thank-you note?

Lingering with a friend?

Helping an elderly parent or grandparent with shopping?

Letting go of something on your agenda to spend quality time
with your child?

Ask God to help you trust that He will return your time in full
measure.

God's Greatest Gift

♥

We praise God for the glorious grace He has poured out on us who
belong to His dear Son. He is so rich in kindness and grace that He
purchased our freedom with the blood of His Son and forgave our sins.
EPHESIANS 1:6-7

Read the above verses again slowly; then think about how generous God has been in forgiving you.

How might this encourage you to generously show others mercy, grace, and forgiveness? Is there someone specific who comes to mind to whom you can show mercy and forgiveness, even though they don't deserve it?

In the past week, which exercise has been most difficult for you? Being generous with your money? Talents? Time? Home? Possessions?

Spend a few minutes talking to God about this. Ask Him to challenge you to continue giving in this area so you can keep growing in generosity.

WEEK 19

Seeing What Others Don't

♥

We don't look at the troubles we can see now; rather, we fix our
gaze on things that cannot be seen. For the things we see now
will soon be gone, but the things we cannot see will last forever.

2 CORINTHIANS 4:18

Humans suffer from shortsightedness. We focus on today's tasks
and tomorrow's problems. But God offers a different perspective,
urging us to make each day an investment in eternity. We are to
think about heaven (Colossians 3:2), store up treasures in heaven
(Matthew 6:20), and "live as citizens of heaven" (Philippians 1:27).

Developing an eternal perspective helps us view life differently by reminding us to invest in what will last forever. It gives us
strength to persevere through trials because we know this life is
not our final destination. The more focused we are on our eternal
future with Jesus, the less attached we become to our own desires
and plans and to the temporary attractions of this world.

This week, allow yourself to meditate on the beautiful future
God has for you in eternity and notice how it affects your attitudes,
choices, and relationships.

Who Would Have Dreamed?

❤

No eye has seen, no ear has heard, and no mind has
imagined what God has prepared for those who love Him.
1 CORINTHIANS 2:9

Write this verse down and put it in a visible place so you can meditate upon it throughout the week.

Remember to read it slowly each day and reflect on how its message can change how you think and what you do. Allow your mind to imagine what God has waiting for you.

Homesick for Heaven

❤

Do not love this world nor the things it offers you, for when you
love the world, you do not have the love of the Father in you.
For the world offers only a craving for physical pleasure,
a craving for everything we see, and pride in our achievements
and possessions. These are not from the Father, but are from
this world. And this world is fading away, along with everything that
people crave. But anyone who does what pleases God will live forever.

1 JOHN 2:15–17

What do you most long for? A new car? A different job? A spouse
or a child?

Have you considered that what you truly long for is the person
you were made for? We were made to be with Jesus and live with
Him in heaven.

How might your present longing actually be a form of home-
sickness for heaven?

Heavenly Bodies

♥

We know that when this earthly tent we live in is taken down
(that is, when we die and leave this earthly body), we will have a
house in heaven, an eternal body made for us by God Himself
and not by human hands. We grow weary in our present bodies,
and we long to put on our heavenly bodies like new clothing.

2 CORINTHIANS 5:1-2

Take a few moments and tune in to your earthly body.

Are you physically weary?

Where are your aches and pains?

What traumas have taken a toll on your body?

Now imagine coming face-to-face with Jesus to receive a new,
heavenly body. What might it feel like to "put on" that body like
new clothing?

What part of your earthly body are you most eager to leave
behind?

What parts of your heavenly body are you most excited to
experience?

What If It Were Today?

♥

Those who use the things of the world should not become
attached to them. For this world as we know it will soon pass away.

1 CORINTHIANS 7:31

How would you feel if you knew Jesus would be coming back today? In complete honesty, is there any part of leaving this world that would make you sad?

Perhaps not getting married?

Not being able to watch your children grow up?

Having your hard-earned career cut short?

Never traveling to a place you've always wanted to see?

This exercise is hard because your feelings may be focused on family and friends.

Even so, ask God if you might be overattached to certain aspects of your life. End your meditation time by referring to 1 Corinthians 2:9.

No More

♥

He will wipe every tear from their eyes, and there will be no more
death or sorrow or crying or pain. All these things are gone forever.

REVELATION 21:4

Take a moment to think about what it would feel like to never again
experience death, sorrow, crying, or pain.

What would it be like to never again have to say good-bye to
loved ones? To never have your heart broken or experience a deep
loss?

Consider how this future reality might give you perspective
and encourage you in your present troubles.

Face-to-Face

♥

> When I saw Him, I fell at his feet as if I were dead. But He laid
> His right hand on me and said, "Don't be afraid! I am the First
> and the Last. I am the living One. I died, but look—I am alive
> forever and ever! And I hold the keys of death and the grave."
>
> **REVELATION 1:17–18**

Think about your life with Jesus so far.

What have been your most cherished times together?

In what season did He feel most close?

In what season did He feel most far away?

When did you obey the hardest command He ever gave you?

What was your most intimate time of prayer?

Now reflect on what it will be like to see Jesus with your own eyes for the first time.

What are you both going to talk about when you are face-to-face?

WEEK 20

The Test

♥

My purpose in writing is to encourage you and
assure you that what you are experiencing is truly part
of God's grace for you. Stand firm in this grace.

1 PETER 5:12

One of the most challenging tests the Lord may give us is the opportunity to trust in His faithfulness during difficult times. We fail at these tests when we lose perspective about God's bigger plans for us.

That's why it is important to continually strengthen the spiritual muscle of steadfastness. Steadfastness means learning to endure patiently in faith, or having "courage stretched out." Because life is full of adversity, we will have many opportunities to practice this discipline. Although God sometimes delivers His people from difficult circumstances, He often calls us to courageous and enduring faithfulness in the midst of trials.

If you are in a difficult season, the Holy Spirit has orchestrated the timing of this week just for you. If you are in a season of joy and blessing, simply be uplifted by God this week so that when tough times do come, you will be better prepared to face them with courage.

God at Work in You

♥

I am certain that God, who began the good work
within you, will continue His work until it is finally
finished on the day when Christ Jesus returns.

PHILIPPIANS 1:6

Write down the phrase *God will continue His good work in me* on
three sticky notes and put them in three visible spots around your
home—on the bathroom mirror, on your bedside table, over the
kitchen sink, etc.

Whenever you read them, remind yourself that God is always
at work in you, even if you feel powerless to persevere.

When There Is No Way Out

♥

*We think you ought to know … about the trouble we went through
in the province of Asia. We were crushed and overwhelmed
beyond our ability to endure, and we thought we would never live
through it. In fact, we expected to die. But as a result, we stopped relying
on ourselves and learned to rely only on God, who raises the dead.*

2 CORINTHIANS 1:8-9

Recall a problem in which you felt you had no way out. How did God reveal Himself during that time?

What is the biggest trial confronting you now?

To exercise your need to rely on God, kneel in prayer and clench your fists.

Now slowly open your hands, palms up, as a symbol of releasing your problem to God.

Ask Him to help you wait patiently, and watch how He will work in this situation.

The Upside of Doubt

♥

When doubts filled my mind, Your comfort
gave me renewed hope and cheer.
PSALM 94:19

In what areas are you tempted to doubt God?

Perhaps you struggle to believe that He really cares about you, that He wants the best for you, or that your problems matter to Him.

Take some time to really think about it. How do these struggles impact your ability to persevere in your faith?

Doubt can actually be a blessing if it leads you to honestly search for a better understanding of who God is. Allow your doubts to lead you back to the Lord.

Each time you find yourself doubting God, use it as a reminder to pray. Ask Him to transform your thoughts of doubt into thoughts of hope.

Strength to Keep Going

With this news, strengthen those who have tired hands,
and encourage those who have weak knees.

ISAIAH 35:3

God, who encourages those who are discouraged,
encouraged us by the arrival of Titus.

2 CORINTHIANS 7:6

Whom has God put in your life to encourage you and give you strength to keep going?

Call or text them right now and ask them to pray that the Lord will replace any feelings of doubt or discouragement in your heart with hope and joy.

Be encouraged that you have trusted friends or family members who are praying for you throughout this day.

A God-Sized Compliment

❤

I know all the things you do. I have seen your love,
your faith, your service, and your patient endurance.
And I can see your constant improvement in all these things.

REVELATION 2:19

Imagine God speaking these words to you. What specific things would He tell you He sees and is proud of?

Your work ethic?

Your care for your family or friends?

Your desire to grow closer to Him?

How does it make you feel to be understood and encouraged by the God of the universe?

Remember that as you strive to practice the discipline of steadfastness, God sees you and is proud of you.

The Best Way to Grow

♥

When your faith is tested, your endurance has a chance to grow.
So let it grow, for when your endurance is fully developed,
you will be perfect and complete, needing nothing.
JAMES 1:3-4

As difficult as it may be, spend a few moments thanking God for a trial in your life.

How did it help you grow?

What are some ways it made you rely more on Him?

Did it end up turning your life in a different direction that was better than your original plan?

Ask God to use this time to strengthen you for future tests of faith.

And as you conclude these exercises in being steadfast in your faith, reflect on which exercise most encouraged you toward patient endurance and courageous trust in God.

WEEK 21

Poor Connections

❦

Don't copy the behavior and customs of this world, but let God transform
you into a new person by changing the way you think. Then you will learn
to know God's will for you, which is good and pleasing and perfect.

ROMANS 12:2

Jesus often withdrew from crowds and busyness to be with His Father. If Jesus thought it essential to "unplug," how much more ought we to do the same in an age of mass communication and technology?

We live with constant interruptions, and as a result, we have become distracted, poor listeners, and unable to connect deeply with others. Unplugging is detaching from routine distractions, especially technology, to be fully present with God and others. Unplugging will take effort and intentionality, but it is important for our spiritual growth and relationship with God.

This week will focus primarily on helping you assess your use and need of technology and how it impacts your relationships. You may feel uncomfortable letting go of being "connected." When you are tempted to reconnect too soon, focus instead on your connection with God.

The Weight of Technology

♥

Let us strip off every weight that slows us down, especially
the sin that so easily trips us up. And let us run with endurance
the race God has set before us. We do this by keeping our
eyes on Jesus, the champion who initiates and perfects our faith.

HEBREWS 12:1–2

Read this verse again—slowly.

Now think about your use of technology.

How often does it slow you down spiritually?

Cause you to sin?

Take your focus off Jesus?

Ask the Lord how He would like you to be more intentional
this week about unplugging.

For example, perhaps you could replace social media with
prayer or put all technology in another room when you read your
Bible.

Doing so may help you better keep your eyes on Him.

Fixed Thoughts

♥

Fix your thoughts on what is true, and honorable,
and right, and pure, and lovely, and admirable.
Think about things that are excellent and worthy of praise.
PHILIPPIANS 4:8

How does social media impact your thought life?

This week, keep a journal of what your thoughts are fixed on after spending time on social media.

Does it tempt you to sin by comparing and coveting?

Does it distract you from thinking about things that are worthy of God's praise?

Every time you finish using social media, jot down these thoughts.

Now set a reminder for the end of the week to talk to the Lord about your observations.

What Is Truly Life-Giving?

♥

Be careful how you live. Don't live like fools, but like those who
are wise. Make the most of every opportunity in these evil days.
EPHESIANS 5:15-16

Schedule a time to go out in public this week just to observe how others use technology.

Go to a coffee shop, the park, or even the lobby after church. How many people are on their phones instead of talking to the person they are with?

Read the verses again with your own life in mind. After observing the use of technology in a public place, how do you think the Lord might be calling you to set aside your own devices in order to make the most of every opportunity?

Quiet Spaces

♥

I have calmed and quieted myself, like a weaned child who no longer cries
for its mother's milk. Yes, like a weaned child is my soul within me.
PSALM 131:2

Go for a walk or run an errand today without your phone. Use
this time to calm and quiet your soul without the temptation of
looking at your phone.

As you walk, pray about what it feels like for you to be without
your phone during this time.

Is it freeing?

Do you feel insecure?

Are there any kinds of fears associated with not being connected?

Face-to-Face

♥

Do to others as you would like them to do to you.
LUKE 6:31

How does it make you feel when someone gives you his or her undivided attention?

Choose one way to connect with another person "face-to-face" today:

- Invite someone for coffee without the interruptions of technology.
- Play a game with your family instead of watching TV.
- Send a handwritten letter, instead of an email, to a friend.

As you do this, reflect on how it feels to connect more personally, and think about the negative impact technology may be having on your relationships.

Saying No to Technology Slavery

♥

You say, "I am allowed to do anything"—
but not everything is good for you.
And even though "I am allowed to do anything,"
I must not become a slave to anything.
1 CORINTHIANS 6:12

Choose two hours today to unplug fully. Shut off your phone, turn off the TV, and refrain from using the computer.

Use some of this time to be with the Lord and reflect on the above verse. What has this time revealed to you about the way technology enslaves you?

As you reflect on the past seven days, consider whether unplugging has revealed any ways in which you have copied the behaviors of this world.

How might God be calling you to change the way you think about technology?

Ask Him to help you unplug more and more for the sake of your thoughts, heart, relationships, and prayer life.

WEEK 22

MAY 28

Don't Miss Out

❤

Jacob awoke from his sleep and said,
"Surely the Lord is in this place, and I wasn't even aware of it!"
GENESIS 28:16

Too often we live our days on autopilot—being physically there but not really being *present*. In *Here and Now*, Henri Nouwen explains the power of being present by stating, "The real enemies of our life are the 'oughts' and the 'ifs.' They pull us backward into the unalterable past and forward into the unpredictable future. But real life takes place in the here and the now."[13]

Being present means waking up to the world around us so we don't miss God's gifts. This isn't meant to be practiced only in good times, but in difficult times too. God is always at work and has gifts for us that are just waiting to be unwrapped.

These gifts are harder to see in difficult seasons, and we won't find them by living in the past or looking to the future. So whether we are in a season of joy or sorrow, we can see every moment as an opportunity to discover and unwrap the wonderful gifts God has for us in the present.

Where Are You?

❤

The thief's purpose is to steal and kill and destroy.
My purpose is to give them a rich and satisfying life.
JOHN 10:10

Don't allow Satan to steal moments from your day.

Set an alarm or a reminder on your phone, and when it goes off, ask yourself these questions:

- *Am I being present with the people around me?*
- *Am I daydreaming instead of listening to someone?*
- *Am I wishing I were somewhere other than where I am?*

Make it a habit to ask God to help you be aware of the rich and satisfying moments He brings before you every day.

Hidden Treasure

♥

I will give you treasures hidden in the darkness—secret riches.
I will do this so you may know that I am the LORD,
the God of Israel, the One who calls you by name.

ISAIAH 45:3

What hardship are you currently facing?

What treasures might God have hidden for you during this dark season?

In difficult times it is especially hard to be present. You may tend either to linger with regret over the past, replaying the circumstances of your hardship, or to dream about the future with a longing for better times.

Instead of wishing for the trial to be over, ask the Lord to help you be cognizant of his presence during this difficult time.

What might He be doing in your life right now?

What gifts might He be offering you in the present?

Present at the Table

♥

I decided there is nothing better than to enjoy food and drink and
to find satisfaction in work. Then I realized that these pleasures are
from the hand of God. For who can eat or enjoy anything apart from Him?

ECCLESIASTES 2:24-25

How often do you multitask while you eat?

Do you check emails on your phone while having lunch with someone, for instance, or watch TV during dinner?

Practice being present today by taking time to smell and taste your food. Chew slowly. Enjoy each flavor as it hits your tongue.

How does this way of eating help you better enjoy God's gift of food?

Soak It In

♥

Children born to a young man are like arrows in a warrior's hands.
How joyful is the man whose quiver is full of them!
PSALM 127:4-5

Think about the people you are going to see today, and thank God for each person you interact with.

When you are with your family and friends (or even those who are difficult to be around), take a moment to soak in this privilege of being with each person God has placed in your life.

You never know how long you will have someone, so when you are with them, enjoy them!

Breathe In, Breathe Out

♥

The Spirit of God has made me,
and the breath of the Almighty gives me life.
JOB 33:4

Close your eyes and spend the next few minutes focusing on your breathing.

Breathe deeply and slowly.

Pay attention to the sound of your heartbeat, the rising and falling of your chest, and the space of waiting in between each breath.

Simply receive this time as a gift and allow yourself to relax fully.

Now read this verse again as you thank God for making you and putting breath in your lungs at this very moment.

Sense the Moment

♥

Since everything God created is good,
we should not reject any of it but receive it with thanks.
1 TIMOTHY 4:4–5

Practice being present by allowing your five senses to help you be in the moment.

What do you see, smell, taste, and hear?

What kinds of sensations do you feel against your skin?

Several times during the day, stop for a few moments and ask these five questions.

Become more alive to God's world around you. Thank Him for the gift of your senses and reflect on the fact that each moment is unique and special.

Now think back over the past several days you spent practicing being more present.

When did you feel most present with God and others?

When were you most absent from God and others?

WEEK 23

Can You Hear Him?

Listen to me! For I have important things to tell you.
PROVERBS 8:6

God calls us to be "quick to listen, slow to speak, and slow to get angry" (James 1:19). Sadly, too often we are slow to listen, quick to speak, and quick to get angry. Listening is an art and one that is close to God's heart.

Since God always listens to us, we minister to others by listening to them. Listening is a form of love. We show others they are valuable when we listen with respect, care, and patience, and when we refrain from interrupting with our own thoughts and advice. We must set aside our schedules and distractions to be fully present and to hear every word that is being spoken. *Really* listening takes practice and will not be mastered in a week.

The exercises this week will reveal your current listening habits. God may use some of these exercises to show you how you could lovingly listen better—both to Him and to others. Be encouraged that God is shaping your heart to love others well through the ministry of listening.

Come and Listen

♥

Come and listen to my counsel.
I'll share my heart with you and make you wise.
PROVERBS 1:23

My sheep listen to My voice;
I know them, and they follow Me.
JOHN 10:27

What does the voice of God sound like to you?

Is it accepting or condemning?

Demanding or gentle?

Loud or silent?

Ask God right now to help you hear His voice more clearly this week as you practice listening.

Make an effort to write down anything you hear God tell you as you practice the discipline of listening.

Listen and Learn

♥

If you listen to correction, you grow in understanding.
PROVERBS 15:32

You must all be quick to listen, slow to speak, and slow to get angry.
JAMES 1:19

Ask a trusted, honest family member or close friend whether you have been a good listener to them in the past.

Do you give them space to talk?

Does your body language show you are engaged?

Do you ask questions that reflect you have heard and understood what they have been saying?

Sometimes good listening requires self-restraint, so welcome their feedback by listening without interrupting, getting defensive, or trying to explain yourself.

Listening to God's Word

♥

Jesus replied, "But even more blessed are all who
hear the word of God and put it into practice."
LUKE 11:28

How often do you listen to God's Word when you read it?

As you practice listening this week, read each day's Scripture slowly, as if God is speaking it directly to you.

Take time to pause and listen after you have read His Word. Pray, "God, what might You want to speak to me through this verse?"

As you practice listening to God's Word, remind yourself that if God is speaking to you, you won't want to miss it!

Stop and Listen

♥

Don't look out only for your own interests,
but take an interest in others, too.
PHILIPPIANS 2:4

When you ask someone, "How are you?" do you actually stop to listen to their answer?

Or do you tend to rush right past them?

Are you so busy thinking about what you will say next that you don't even listen to what the other person is saying?

Practice listening to someone today by asking them, "How is your day going?" and then taking an interest in what they say, giving them your full attention.

Speak, O Lord

♥

[Eli] said to Samuel, "Go and lie down again, and if someone calls again, say, 'Speak, LORD, Your servant is listening.'" So Samuel went back to bed. And the LORD came and called as before, "Samuel! Samuel!" And Samuel replied, "Speak, Your servant is listening."

1 SAMUEL 3:9–10

When was the last time you heard the Lord speak to you? Create space to hear God by setting a reminder on your bedside table to rest in the quiet with Him before you fall asleep.

Simply pray, "Lord, what do You want to say to me about this past day? About tomorrow?" Lie in the quiet and reflect on anything (absolutely anything!) that comes to mind.

Ask yourself whether the words you hear might be from the Lord. Do they align with Scripture? Are they words spoken in love and grace? Do they point you toward God and His Kingdom?

Listening with Your Mouth

Spouting off before listening to the facts is both shameful
and foolish.... The tongue can bring death or life;
those who love to talk will reap the consequences.

PROVERBS 18:13, 21

Read the above passage again carefully and ask God whether this
is something you struggle with in listening.

Do you tend to spout off before gaining the facts of the whole
story?

Do you love to talk more than listen?

Is it more difficult for you to listen to certain people or in
specific situations?

Ask forgiveness for ways you have failed to listen well to
others, and receive God's grace.

As you've practiced the art of listening these past few days,
what have you learned about the way you listen to God and others?

WEEK 24

The Best Example to Follow

♥

How precious are Your thoughts about me,
O God. They cannot be numbered!

PSALM 139:17

Live a life filled with love, following the example of Christ.

EPHESIANS 5:2

We can easily become wrapped up in our own lives and miss the needs around us. How do we change our focus to be more oriented toward the needs of others?

Practicing thoughtfulness helps us grow more considerate and attentive to the feelings and needs of those around us. Thoughtfulness, like listening, is a form of love. God's Word calls us to love others by looking for opportunities to do good for them.

The exercises this week aim to make thoughtfulness a regular way of relating to others in your life. Some will be as simple as offering a kind word, asking an insightful question, or giving someone the benefit of the doubt. Allow the Lord to lead you in big or small ways as you develop the habit of thoughtfulness over the next several days.

How Thoughtful Are You?

♥

Let's not get tired of doing what is good. At just the right
time we will reap a harvest of blessing if we don't give up.
Therefore, whenever we have the opportunity, we should
do good to everyone—especially to those in the family of faith.

GALATIANS 6:9-10

Can you give an honest assessment of your thoughtfulness? On a scale from one to ten (one being "not at all thoughtful," and ten being "extremely thoughtful"), how would you rate yourself overall?

Does it come naturally for you to do good to others, or do you need to work at it?

Do you often forget family members' and friends' birthdays and milestones?

Ask God to open your eyes to see and your heart to respond to opportunities for practicing thoughtfulness toward others this week.

JUNE 13

Thoughtful Questions

♥

*When Jesus saw him and knew he had been ill for
a long time, He asked him, "Would you like to get well?"*
JOHN 5:6

Jesus often asked thoughtful questions that spoke to a person's real needs.

Think of three people with whom you are close and come up with a thoughtful question that speaks to each one's real needs (for example, if someone has been going through a stressful time, asking them if this week has been any better).

Then be sure to ask each of them! If you have trouble thinking of a question, think about what you would want others to ask you.

Consider What's Best

♥

I, too, try to please everyone in everything I do. I don't just do what
is best for me; I do what is best for others so that many may be saved.
1 CORINTHIANS 10:33

Take a moment to ask the Lord if there is anything in your life that
might cause another person to sin or stumble.

Have you been bragging about something you've accomplished?

Complaining about something you don't have?

Grumbling about something you do have that someone else
longs for?

Engaging in a habit that is a struggle for someone else?

You will know you have grown in thoughtfulness if the next
time you are with that person, you think about them first before
speaking or acting.

Your Love Language

♥

Love each other with genuine affection,
and take delight in honoring each other.

ROMANS 12:10

Author Gary Chapman is perhaps best known for his wonderful book *The Five Love Languages*.

Choose someone close to you and consider which of the five love languages fits them best: acts of service, quality time, words of affirmation, physical touch, or gifts. If you don't know what their love language is, simply ask.

Prayerfully consider with the Lord how to honor this person this week by loving them in the way they would best receive it.

Thinking Better

♥

Always be humble and gentle. Be patient with each other,
making allowance for each other's faults because of your love.

EPHESIANS 4:2

Read this verse once more while thinking of someone who has recently offended you—whether they realized it or not. Today your exercise is to give them the benefit of the doubt.

For example, if another driver cut you off, could it be because they were late to something important?

Maybe they didn't see you?

Or maybe they just had a bad day?

This may be a hard exercise if someone has intentionally hurt you. Remember that most people who try to hurt others do it because they have been hurt themselves.

This exercise is not about excusing their behavior but rather about changing the way you see and think about them.

JUNE 17

Do It

♥

Don't be concerned for your own good but for the good of others.
1 CORINTHIANS 10:24

Whom do you know who is experiencing a trial or is in a difficult season?

Write down three things to encourage them this week. It could be something as involved as taking them a meal, or something as quick as sending an encouraging text. But do one of those three things today to keep practicing the act of thoughtfulness.

Think back over the past seven days of practicing thoughtfulness. How has it felt to engage in exercises that asked you to intentionally think of others? How might your sacrifices have pleased God over the past week? How might they have strengthened your relationships with others?

WEEK 25

Guard Your Lips

Take control of what I say, O LORD, and guard my lips.
PSALM 141:3

Do you have a tendency to say things you later regret? Are there times you wish you'd just kept your mouth shut? Do you complain too much, gossip, use profanity, or criticize others?

If these things describe you, then you may have a problem controlling your tongue. Controlling your tongue is being aware of what comes out of your mouth and then, by the Holy Spirit's power, changing words that are destructive into those that are gracious, thankful, encouraging, loving, truthful, and a blessing to others. God emphasizes that even though the tongue is small, it holds incredible power. It can be used to praise God and bless others. But if not controlled, it can set one's whole life on fire (see James 3:5-6).

The exercises this week will ask you to reflect on what comes out of your mouth. Controlling the tongue is a practice that takes a lifetime to learn, and you will continually need God's help with it.

What Can You Say?

If you claim to be religious but don't control your tongue,
you are fooling yourself, and your religion is worthless.
JAMES 1:26

If you have a problem controlling your tongue, you are probably aware of it because you may have repeatedly hurt family and friends with your words.

What can you do to be more intentional about controlling your tongue? Think of one thing to practice today, such as *I will not speak if I am angry, I will ask a question before making a comment, I will start each conversation with a compliment,* or *I will count to three before I say anything.*

As you practice this exercise of changing your speech, ask the Lord to also change your heart to be more gracious to others.

Filing Your Complaints

---

*Do everything without complaining and arguing, so that no one
can criticize you. Live clean, innocent lives as children of God,
shining like bright lights in a world full of crooked and perverse people.*
PHILIPPIANS 2:14–15

Be mindful of when you are tempted to complain today. If you catch yourself complaining, text the letter *C* to yourself or tally your complaints on a piece of paper.

At the end of the day, count how many times you have texted or written that letter. Ask for God's forgiveness and thank Him that you are beginning to practice controlling your tongue.

Make a commitment that tomorrow, each time you want to complain, you will say something to express thankfulness in that situation, and remind yourself how words make a real difference in your attitude and relationships.

Truth Teller

———— ♥ ————

Some people make cutting remarks, but the words of the wise bring healing.
Truthful words stand the test of time, but lies are soon exposed....
The Lᴏʀᴅ detests lying lips, but He delights in those who tell the truth.
PROVERBS 12:18-19, 22

————

The truth is that we don't always like to tell the truth because it exposes our motives, it can make us look bad in front of others, and it forces us to be accountable.

In what situations are you most tempted to exaggerate, stretch the truth, or tell a little white lie? Commit to telling the truth no matter what the potential consequences to you.

While the short-term consequences of consistent truth telling might sometimes be painful, the long-term outcome will be deep relationships with others because they can always trust you. And remember that God will honor your honesty.

Words of Encouragement

❤

Let us think of ways to motivate one another to acts of love and
good works. And let us not neglect our meeting together,
as some people do, but encourage one another,
especially now that the day of his return is drawing near.
HEBREWS 10:24-25

Ask God to bring to mind a person who would be blessed by your words today.

Whom do you think of first?

What kinds of words would make them feel special, loved, and encouraged in Christ?

Take a few minutes to write that person an encouraging note by hand, and mail it to them today.

The Weapon of Peace

♥

The LORD will fight for you, and you have only to be silent.
EXODUS 14:14, ESV

God blesses those who work for peace,
for they will be called the children of God.
MATTHEW 5:9

How often do you feel tempted to use words as a weapon?

Ask the Lord if there is an area in your life where He might be calling you to step back and be silent.

Or perhaps there is a situation in which you can work to be a peacemaker with your words.

What comes to mind?

What can you do today to use your words to bring peace to a person or situation?

Loose Language

♥

[Jesus said,] "I tell you this, you must give an account
on judgment day for every idle word you speak.
The words you say will either acquit you or condemn you."

MATTHEW 12:36–37

Don't use foul or abusive language. Let everything
you say be good and helpful, so that your words
will be an encouragement to those who hear them.

EPHESIANS 4:29

When was the last time you used profanity?

What caused you to do it?

An argument? Another driver? Stubbing your toe or hitting
your head on something?

Or has bad language slowly become a normal part of your
speech?

If so, confess this to the Lord. Now commit not to use any
profanity for the rest of the day. Keep practicing until it is no
longer part of your speech.

WEEK 26

Lift Up Another

♥

Dear brothers and sisters, pray for us.
1 THESSALONIANS 5:25

Do you ever say you will pray for someone and then forget to do it? How often do you pray for believers around the world? For the leaders of your country? For your church?

God's Word urges us to pray for *all* people (see 1 Timothy 2:1). Praying for others means going before the Lord on their behalf. This requires humility because it causes us to set aside our own agendas in prayer to lift up someone else to our heavenly Father.

We may never know the outcome of our prayers in this lifetime, but God promises that our earnest prayers have great power and produce wonderful results (see James 5:16).

This week will stretch you to pray for others in your home, in your neighborhood, and across the globe. Some exercises will challenge you to pray for people you may not want to pray for. Ask God to give you a heart of compassion toward them. Trust that He will use your prayers to produce wonderful results you never thought possible.

Pray for Your Leaders

❤

Pray for all people. Ask God to help them; intercede on their
behalf, and give thanks for them. Pray this way for kings and
all who are in authority so that we can live peaceful and quiet
lives marked by godliness and dignity. This is good and pleases God
our Savior, who wants everyone to be saved and to understand the truth.

1 TIMOTHY 2:1-4

Spend some time today praying for those in authority or those
who have power over your country. Use the above verse as a model
for how to pray for them.

Pray for the Persecuted

♥

Bless those who persecute you.
Don't curse them; pray that God will bless them.
ROMANS 12:14

Stay alert and be persistent in your
prayers for all believers everywhere.
EPHESIANS 6:18

Go online and find sources that list the top countries where Christians are being persecuted.

Ask God which country He would like you to pray for over the next week. Write a note to remind yourself to pray for this country every day.

Pray for those being persecuted within that country as well as for those who are persecuting them.

Pray for a Place of Sacred Impact

♥

[Solomon prayed,] "May you watch over this Temple night and day,
this place where You have said, 'My name will be there.' May You always hear
the prayers I make toward this place. May You hear the humble and earnest
requests from me and Your people Israel when we pray toward this place.
Yes, hear us from heaven where You live, and when You hear, forgive."

1 KINGS 8:29-30

Pray in the Spirit at all times and on every occasion.

EPHESIANS 6:18

Go on a prayer walk with the Lord. Walk slowly through a place,
such as your home, neighborhood, or church, and intentionally
pray for that place and the people coming to and going from it.

Pray for Friends and Family

♥

While Peter was in prison, the church prayed very earnestly for him.
ACTS 12:5

We have not stopped praying for you since we first heard about you.
We ask God to give you complete knowledge of His will and
to give you spiritual wisdom and understanding.
COLOSSIANS 1:9

It is easy to tell people we will pray for them and then neglect to do it.

Text or call someone today and ask how you can pray for them this week. Then remember to do it!

Remind yourself to follow up with them later about their prayer request, and ask them if they would like you to continue to pray.

Pray for Your Enemy

♥

You have heard the law that says, "Love your neighbor" and hate your enemy.
But I say, love your enemies! Pray for those who persecute you!
In that way, you will be acting as true children of your Father in heaven.

MATTHEW 5:43-45

Is there anyone whom you would consider your "enemy" or who is very difficult to love?

Use the questions below to help you prepare to pray for this person. Ask the Lord,

- What do You want my prayer to be for this person?
- Is there anything in me that is getting in the way of praying for this person?
- Is there anything You want me to say or do on behalf of this person that would reflect Your love for them?

Pray for God's Will in the World

♥

The Father who knows all hearts knows what the Spirit is saying,
for the Spirit pleads for us believers in harmony with God's own will.

ROMANS 8:27

Look through a newspaper, watch the news, or search online for important events happening around the world today. Ask God whom He might be calling you to pray for right now.

As you conclude your week of praying for others, look back over the people you prayed for. Take a moment to think about what it will be like to watch God answer your prayers for friends and family.

Then imagine being in heaven one day, meeting people whom you prayed for without knowing them personally, and hearing how God answered your prayers for them.

WEEK 27

JULY 2

Step into It

♥

Be happy with those who are happy, and weep with those who weep.
ROMANS 12:15

Our world is full of people who desperately need to experience the compassion of Jesus. Since Christ is always loving, tender, and sympathetic toward us, how can we not be the same toward others?

Compassion means opening your heart to those hurting around you and then doing something about it. It is both an emotion (feeling concern for someone) and an action (doing something to meet their need). Compassion compels you to intentionally step into the pain of the world, instead of trying to avoid it. You can't force yourself to feel compassion, but it is possible to put your heart in the right posture to notice and sympathize with the hurt all around you.

The exercises this week ask you to reflect on God's compassion toward you and then to imagine yourself in the shoes of those in need. Ask the Lord to change you into someone who notices the pain in the eyes of others, who is sensitive to unspoken needs, and who is always ready to serve.

Receiving God's Compassion

♥

You must be compassionate, just as your Father is compassionate.
LUKE 6:36

Begin this week by reflecting on the ways God has shown compassion to you. How has He:

- cared for you during a desperate time (see Genesis 16:13)?
- loved you even in your worst times of sin (see Romans 5:8)?
- comforted you in the midst of your pain (see Psalm 34:18)?
- healed your broken heart (see Psalm 147:3)?
- given you a chance to start over (see Lamentations 3:22-23)?
- met one of your deepest needs (see Philippians 4:19)?

How might this encourage you to show the same kind of compassion to others?

Comfort Others

♥

All praise to God, the Father of our Lord Jesus Christ. God is our merciful Father and the source of all comfort. He comforts us in all our troubles so that we can comfort others. When they are troubled, we will be able to give them the same comfort God has given us.

2 CORINTHIANS 1:3-4

Today, practice compassion by comforting someone who needs it.

For example, if your friend is worried about losing her job, think about what she might be feeling.

Pressure? Fear? Anxiety?

Take time to listen, sympathize, and offer compassionate statements, such as "It sounds like you are feeling a lot of pressure," or "It seems like you're feeling a lot of fear right now."

Do not try to fix anything or dole out advice when you offer comfort; just be a compassionate listener.

Who Needs You Today?

—— ♥ ——

If someone has enough money to live well and sees a brother or sister in
need but shows no compassion—how can God's love be in that person?

1 JOHN 3:17

Think of one immediate need around you today. Perhaps a sick
friend needs a meal, a lonely person could use a friend, or a
homeless person needs a blanket.

Imagine yourself in that situation. What might they be feeling
right now?

Ask God how you can act on meeting this need today (or this
week), and then make sure you follow through.

It's important to ask God before you act, because there may be
times when He will put into your mind just the right way to serve
the person in need.

Compassion to All

♥

The Lord is good to everyone. He showers compassion on all His creation.

PSALM 145:9

Do you believe some people deserve compassion more than others?

How do you feel about showing compassion toward those whom you see as lazy, rude, arrogant, vulgar, or wealthy?

Read the above passage again and reflect on the words *everyone* and *all*. Talk to the Lord about someone who comes to mind who doesn't seem to deserve your compassion.

How might God be asking you to show compassion to this person today?

Perhaps it could be through an act of kindness, praying for the Lord to work in your own heart, or simply putting yourself in their shoes.

Compassion in the Home

Be kind to each other, tenderhearted, forgiving
one another, just as God through Christ has forgiven you.
EPHESIANS 4:32

Think of a family member who has been unkind, critical, or offensive toward you. Practice compassion by putting yourself in their position and then thinking about these questions:

- How do you think it would feel to be this person?
- What hardships have they faced in life?
- How might their own unmet needs impact the way they interact with you?

Reflect on how God has shown you compassion. Spend the next few minutes praying for this person.

Compassion toward Your Community

♥

A man with leprosy came and knelt in front of Jesus,
begging to be healed. "If you are willing, you can heal me
and make me clean," he said. Moved with compassion, Jesus
reached out and touched him. "I am willing," He said. "Be healed!"

MARK 1:40-41

How willing are you to reach out to the outcasts or disenfranchised in your community—for example, the sick, the homeless, the elderly, or the criminals?

How might God be calling you outside your comfort zone to show compassion in one of these areas?

Perhaps by writing a letter to an inmate, taking flowers to a nursing home, serving food at a homeless shelter, or donating to a food pantry?

If you are not able to do something today, schedule a time in the upcoming weeks to serve with your family or friends.

WEEK 28

We Need Each Other

When we get together, I want to encourage you in your faith,
but I also want to be encouraged by yours.

ROMANS 1:12

The discipline of fellowship helps you realize the importance of community in your walk of faith. You need others if you are to grow into the kind of person God wants you to be.

The exercises this week encourage intentionality, authenticity, generosity, and love within the community where God has placed you. If you already have a strong community, many of these exercises will be easy for you. However, if you are still searching for a place of belonging, this week might cause you to feel stretched and uncomfortable. Trust that God will reward your efforts as you seek fellowship in your community.

Real community takes time and a lot of effort, but remember that this week could be the beginning of some beautiful friendships. Doing life with others is not always easy, but with the help of the Holy Spirit, it is one of the best ways to grow and be transformed into Christlikeness.

My Community

♥

We are many parts of one body, and we all belong to each other.

ROMANS 12:5

What role has community played in your life?

Take a few moments to pray over the community that the Lord has placed you in.

Does it feel nurturing or draining?

Do you feel a sense of belonging or isolation?

How does this community lead you closer or further away in your relationship with God?

Today, simply talk to God about what comes to mind as you consider these questions. Ask Him to give you real openness toward fellowship this week.

United in Heart and Mind

All the believers were united in heart and mind. And they felt that
what they owned was not their own, so they shared everything
they had. The apostles testified powerfully to the resurrection
of the Lord Jesus, and God's great blessing was upon them all.

ACTS 4:32–33

Choose one way to model the community of Acts within your own
community this week.

Perhaps you could share your food, space, or time, help a
friend in need, or give away something of yours that you know a
friend needs or would like.

What can you do for someone in your community today?

Build Others Up

♥

Encourage each other and build each other up,
just as you are already doing.
1 THESSALONIANS 5:11

Being intentional to encourage others is an important part of remaining in fellowship.

Whom in your family, workplace, or community can you encourage and build up today?

Ask the Lord which friend He would like you to call, text, or get together with.

Contact that person today to thank them for something they've done, tell them how much you appreciate them, and encourage them in their faith.

Reach Out

❤

All the believers devoted themselves to the apostles'
teaching, and to fellowship, and to sharing in
meals (including the Lord's Supper), and to prayer.
ACTS 2:42

Small groups can be great places to build community.

If you are not part of a small group, ask God if He might be calling you to pursue getting involved in one.

Prayerfully consider a person, couple, or family with whom you would like to connect.

Block out several times on your calendar that would work to meet with them. Then contact them today to ask if any of those times would work to get together.

Peacemaking

♥

If you are presenting a sacrifice at the altar in the Temple and
you suddenly remember that someone has something against you,
leave your sacrifice there at the altar. Go and be reconciled
to that person. Then come and offer your sacrifice to God.

MATTHEW 5:23-24

May God, who gives this patience and encouragement,
help you live in complete harmony with each other,
as is fitting for followers of Christ Jesus.

ROMANS 15:5

Is there someone in your community with whom you are not in
harmony? What steps can you take today to work toward peace
with this person?

Could you apologize for your part in a dispute? Ask for forgiveness? Pray for this person? Work toward a compromise of
some sort?

Consider whether God may be asking you to take the first step
toward reconciliation.

Share Your Burdens

Share each other's burdens, and in this way obey the law of Christ.
GALATIANS 6:2

Being vulnerable with others feels risky, but it is absolutely essential to building and deepening community.

Call or text a safe and trustworthy friend right now and ask them to pray for you.

Try to be more vulnerable than you are comfortable with, staying focused on your own struggles, temptations, and troubles instead of asking for prayers for your family members or friends.

What did it feel like to be encouraging, intentional, authentic, and generous toward your community this week?

Which of these practices might God be asking you to continue for the purpose of deepening your fellowship with others?

WEEK 29

Be a Good Steward

In the beginning God created the heavens and the earth.
GENESIS 1:1

When you are attacking a town and the war drags on ... do not cut
down the trees. Are the trees your enemies, that you should attack them?
DEUTERONOMY 20:19

Caring for creation stands in opposition to today's consumerism and our own selfish desires to live an easy and convenient life. For Christians, caring for creation holds an added significance. It is an outgrowth of our faith, seeing all of God's creation as good and being wise stewards over it. Caring for creation challenges us to practice living within our God-given boundaries by not taking more than we need. It requires us to selflessly love our neighbors as well as future generations by making the earth a better place. It gives us the opportunity to care for something that was meant to glorify God and point people to Him. What an amazing way to participate with God in His work! Ask God to open your heart this week to love and care for creation the way He does.

The World Then and Now

♥

God looked over all He had made, and He saw that it was very good!
And evening passed and morning came, marking the sixth day.

GENESIS 1:31

Imagine yourself in this passage, standing next to God as He looks over His new creation.

What might God have felt toward the earth?

Did He marvel at its beauty?

Did He feel a sense of accomplishment at its amazingly complex design?

Did He feel joy as He listened to the sounds of trees swaying in the breeze, bubbling brooks, croaking frogs, and singing birds?

How do you think God feels when He sees the earth now?

With this picture in mind, ask God to open your heart this week to care more deeply about creation.

Creation Keepers

God said, "Let Us make human beings in Our image,
to be like Us. They will reign over the fish in the sea, the birds
in the sky, the livestock, all the wild animals on the earth,
and the small animals that scurry along the ground."

GENESIS 1:26

What beliefs or habits inhibit you from being a good steward over God's creation?

Is it too inconvenient?

Do you doubt your ability to make a difference?

Does it seem like no one else is doing it?

Think of one thing you can do today to be a better steward of God's creation, such as picking up a piece of litter along your street, turning off the water while brushing your teeth, or recycling.

Plant and Watch

♥

The LORD God placed the man in the
Garden of Eden to tend and watch over it.
GENESIS 2:15

After the flood, Noah began to cultivate
the ground, and he planted a vineyard.
GENESIS 9:20

Abraham planted a tamarisk tree at Beersheba,
and there he worshiped the LORD, the Eternal God.
GENESIS 21:33

This week, plant something either in your yard or in a pot in your home.

Be intentional in caring for it to keep it alive.

What does it feel like to tend and watch over a part of God's creation?

As you care for this plant, use it as a reminder that God has also called you to care for His earth.

God's Care for Animals

♥

The Lord God formed from the ground all the wild animals and all the
birds of the sky. He brought them to the man to see what he would
call them, and the man chose a name for each one. He gave names to
all the livestock, all the birds of the sky, and all the wild animals.
GENESIS 2:19-20

You care for people and animals alike, O Lord.
PSALM 36:6

Read the verses again and think about how God cares for animals.
Search online for a website that lists endangered animals, and
choose one animal to educate yourself on.

Next, reflect on how God must feel to see His creations ceas-
ing to exist. Prayerfully consider how God might be calling you
to care for His animals—perhaps by donating to an organization
that helps endangered species or volunteering at a local animal
shelter.

Creation Renewal

♥

Against its will, all creation was subjected to God's curse.
But with eager hope, the creation looks forward to the day when it
will join God's children in glorious freedom from death and decay.

ROMANS 8:20–21

Walk around your neighborhood or a park and take a small bag so you can pick up any trash you see.

Remember that even if you pick up only one piece of trash, your care of the earth pleases the Lord.

Notice the death and decay around you.

What does it feel like to play a small part in helping restore and care for God's earth?

Shrinking Your Footprint

♥

The earth is the Lord's, and everything in it. The world and
all its people belong to Him. For He laid the earth's
foundation on the seas and built it on the ocean depths.
PSALM 24:1-2

How often do you forget that everything on the earth belongs to
God? Ask Him if He would like you to do something from the
following list as a way to decrease your environmental footprint:

- Walk or bike once in a while instead of driving
- Recycle
- Compost
- Conserve water by only running full dishwashers and washing
  machines
- Turn off lights when you leave a room
- Switch to more energy-efficient lightbulbs
- Use jars or reusable containers instead of plastic bags
- Buy local produce or start growing your own

WEEK 30

Less Is More

Jesus prayed this prayer: "O Father, Lord of heaven and earth,
thank You for hiding these things from those who think
themselves wise and clever, and for revealing them to the childlike."

MATTHEW 11:25

Success is often measured by how much we own and how busy our schedules are. However, God calls His followers to a different way of life—one that resists the "more is better" mentality and instead focuses on our purpose for being on this earth. The practice of simplicity is about letting go of things that clutter and complicate your life in order to keep your focus on the kind of life Jesus says is most fulfilling. Simplicity is not about getting rid of all your things but rather about experiencing freedom from being a slave to them.

This week will challenge you to practice simplicity in multiple areas: your possessions, eating habits, speech, schedules, and relationships. The areas that feel difficult to simplify are likely the areas to which you have become too attached. Allow God to help you experience freedom this week as you refocus on what really matters.

Treasuring Simplicity

♥

[Jesus said,] "Don't store up treasures here on earth, where moths eat them and rust destroys them, and where thieves break in and steal. Store your treasures in heaven, where moths and rust cannot destroy, and thieves do not break in and steal. Wherever your treasure is, there the desires of your heart will also be."

MATTHEW 6:19–21

This week, if a person compliments you on something you own or are wearing, give the item to him or her.

It could be a piece of jewelry or something small in your home.

This is actually a common practice in many cultures.

What does it feel like to give away something you treasure?

Eating Simply

♥

*Not that I was ever in need, for I have learned how to be content
with whatever I have. I know how to live on almost nothing or
with everything. I have learned the secret of living in every situation,
whether it is with a full stomach or empty, with plenty or little.*
PHILIPPIANS 4:11-12

Simplify your eating for the rest of the week.

For example, if you usually have two sides with dinner, limit it to one.

Or if you have meat every night, choose to eat it only one night this week.

Ask the Lord to show you how your eating habits have become excessive or complicated.

Simple as That

♥

Just say a simple, "Yes, I will," or "No, I won't."
Anything beyond this is from the evil one.
MATTHEW 5:37

Read the above verse with your own life in mind.

How often do you say yes and later regret it?

To simplify your life and schedule this week, practice saying no or asking, "Can I get back to you?"

When someone asks you to do something, take time to pray about it before committing to an answer.

This week, your default answer should be "No" unless God is clearly telling you otherwise.

Don't Overcomplicate It

♦

One day an expert in religious law stood up to test Jesus by asking him
this question: "Teacher, what should I do to inherit eternal life?"
Jesus replied, "What does the law of Moses say? How do you read it?"
The man answered, "'You must love the LORD your God with all your
heart, all your soul, all your strength, and all your mind.' And, 'Love your
neighbor as yourself.'" "Right!" Jesus told him. "Do this and you will live!"

LUKE 10:25–28

Think about the simplicity of Jesus' words.

In what ways have you complicated your relationship with
God?

Do you try to work for God's favor?

Are your prayers full of excuses or unnecessary words?

Have certain rituals in your life become more like superstitions?

How might God be using these verses to guide you toward
simplicity in your relationship with Him?

Concern Yourself with One Thing

♥

The Lord said to her, "My dear Martha, you are worried and upset over all these details! There is only one thing worth being concerned about. Mary has discovered it, and it will not be taken away from her."

LUKE 10:41-42

What details are making you fret today?

The clothes you are wearing?

Your messy home?

The amount of money in your bank account?

How might these things be distracting you from focusing on what really matters?

What is the "little" thing you are most anxious about?

Write it on a piece of paper.

Then crumple the paper up and throw it in the garbage as you ask God to free you from your anxiety over this.

Living the Simple Life

♥

Beware! Guard against every kind of greed.
Life is not measured by how much you own.
LUKE 12:15

Take ten minutes today to simplify your possessions. Go through your closet and give away three things you don't often wear—clothing, shoes, belts, scarves.

Or find the things in your garage, closet, or storage area that you keep "just in case," and give one of them away.

This exercise will be a good indicator of how attached you are to your possessions. And it will help you become familiar with your nearest Goodwill, Salvation Army, or other collection center.

How did it feel to simplify your life over the past several days?

Which reflections or exercises freed you up the most?

Ask the Lord how He might want you to continue living simply.

WEEK 31

Take Time to Think

Study this Book of Instruction continually. Meditate on it day and night.
JOSHUA 1:8

In our culture, the word *meditation* has become associated with Eastern spirituality and mysticism. However, the concept of meditation is mentioned throughout the Bible. Joshua talks about meditating on God's law day and night (see Joshua 1:8). David prayed that his meditations would be pleasing to God (see Psalm 19:14). Meditation is mentioned several times in the Psalms (see Psalm 63:6; 145:5). The practice of meditation involves deeply pondering God's Word and what it reveals about Him.

How would your life be different if you strove daily to fill your mind with thoughts about God and His Word? This week will encourage you to think deeply about God's Word, His actions, and His presence in your life. It may be difficult for you to stay focused. Meditation often involves directing and redirecting your thoughts toward God. Take time to read slowly through each Scripture verse. Do your best to let go of the thoughts that preoccupy your mind so that you can better focus on being in God's presence and soaking in His Word.

Meditate on God's Splendor

♥

I will meditate on Your majestic,
glorious splendor and Your wonderful miracles.
PSALM 145:5

Read this verse again slowly and think of a wonderful miracle God has done in your life.

Spend some time reflecting on that experience.

What did you feel in that moment?

What did you learn about God's character?

If you have trouble thinking of a miracle, consider all the ones you may take for granted—for example, think about how your body heals after an injury, or how that "close call" may have been God protecting you, or the miracle of a new baby.

Meditate on God's Word

──────── ♥ ────────

Let all that I am praise the LORD; may I never forget the good things
He does for me. He forgives all my sins and heals all my diseases.
He redeems me from death and crowns me with love and tender mercies.
He fills my life with good things. My youth is renewed like the eagle's!
PSALM 103:2-5

──────────────

Prayerfully and *slowly* read through the passage above three times, using the steps below.

1. The first time you read it, choose one word or phrase that jumps out to you. What made it stand out?
2. During the second reading, ask yourself what you are feeling—either in general or about who God is—as you read this passage.
3. For the third reading, ask the Lord if there is anything He would like to say to you or teach you from this passage.

Meditate on God's Great Deeds

♥

He has given me a new song to sing, a hymn of praise
to our God. Many will see what He has done
and be amazed. They will put their trust in the Lord.

PSALM 40:3

I remember the days of old. I ponder all Your
great works and think about what you have done.

PSALM 143:5

Meditate on three great works God has done in your life.

Take some time to really think about these and write them down. Do you notice any themes in the way He has worked with you?

Meditate on God's Presence

Those who are dominated by the sinful nature think
about sinful things, but those who are controlled by the
Holy Spirit think about things that please the Spirit.

ROMANS 8:5

Set an alarm to go off three times today.

When you hear the alarm, take note of what you are thinking at that moment.

Practice redirecting your thoughts to God and His presence by simply talking to Him about what is on your mind right then.

Ask His Spirit to control your thoughts by reminding you to give them over to God.

This exercise is about training your mind to focus more on God than on things that are less important, or things you know you shouldn't be thinking about.

Meditate on God's Unfailing Love

♥

O God, we meditate on Your unfailing
love as we worship in Your Temple.
PSALM 48:9

O my Strength, to You I sing praises, for You, O God,
are my refuge, the God who shows me unfailing love.
PSALM 59:17

You thrill me, LORD, with all You have done for me!
I sing for joy because of what You have done.
PSALM 92:4

Sing a hymn or worship song to God today (in the shower, in the car, or alone at home).

As you sing the words, meditate on what they say about who God is.

Take notice of how this kind of meditation impacts your attitude throughout the day.

Meditate in Prayer

♥

May the words of my mouth and the meditation
of my heart be pleasing to You,
O Lord, my rock and my redeemer.
PSALM 19:14

Use the Jesus Prayer to help your mind focus exclusively on God and being in His presence. The Jesus Prayer reads, "Jesus Christ, Son of God, have mercy on me, a sinner."

This simple prayer is intended to help you refocus your heart back on God and is based on Luke 17:13, Luke 18:38, and Matthew 6:7-8.

When you pray this prayer, breathe in deeply as you say, "Jesus Christ, Son of God" and slowly exhale as you say, "Have mercy on me, a sinner."

Repeat this prayer several times and allow the words to sink into your heart.

How might this exercise help you focus on God in times of anger, anxiety, or fear?

WEEK 32

AUG. 6

Let Go and Rest

♥

On the seventh day God had finished his work of creation, so he rested from all His work. And God blessed the seventh day and declared it holy, because it was the day when He rested from all His work of creation.

GENESIS 2:2–3

For many, the Sabbath has become a day to catch up on chores or prepare for the week ahead. But God wants you to focus on *rest*.

So why is it so important to take a day off from work?

You need a break from your normal routine in order to enjoy renewal of body, mind, and spirit and to spend time with God and His people.

Keeping Sabbath calls you to set aside one day a week to embrace rest so you have space to worship and enjoy God.

Practicing Sabbath calls you to let go of your busy life and to-do list for twenty-four hours and to trust God with the things left undone.

Since the Sabbath is only one day, the other six days of this week will involve reflection and preparation for the upcoming Sabbath.

What Is Your Sabbath?

Remember to observe the Sabbath day by keeping it holy.
You have six days each week for your ordinary work, but the
seventh day is a Sabbath day of rest dedicated to the Lord your God.
EXODUS 20:8-10

How different does your Sabbath look from the other six days of
the week?

What barriers make it difficult for you to keep the Sabbath?

Busyness?

Work?

Preparing for the upcoming week?

Other obligations?

Take a few moments to have a conversation with the Lord
about this.

You are not trying to come to any conclusions right now; just
talk to God about the Sabbath, why you struggle to keep it, why it is
important to Him, and anything else He brings to mind.

Start the Day with Rest

❤

Work six days only, and rest the seventh; this is to give your oxen
and donkeys a rest, as well as the people of your household.
EXODUS 23:12, TLB

Historically, Sabbath begins at sundown and continues until
sundown of the following day.

Allow this biblical view of time to change the way you begin
and end your days this week. As you fall into bed, view your sleep
as the beginning of a new day.

What thoughts, attitudes, and prayers might God ask you to
"start" each day with as you fall asleep?

Saying Yes to Rest

❤

The Pharisees asked Jesus, "Does the law permit a person to work by healing on the Sabbath?" (They were hoping He would say yes, so they could bring charges against Him.) And He answered, "If you had a sheep that fell into a well on the Sabbath, wouldn't you work to pull it out? Of course you would. And how much more valuable is a person than a sheep! Yes, the law permits a person to do good on the Sabbath."

MATTHEW 12:10-12

Write out a plan to keep the upcoming Sabbath holy and set apart from the rest of the week.

What things do you think God would like you to say yes to on that day—perhaps activities that help restore and reset you?

Worship?

Extended time in God's Word?

Enjoying friends?

Saying No to Busyness

Keep the Sabbath day holy. Don't pursue your own interests on that day,
but enjoy the Sabbath and speak of it with delight as the LORD's holy day.
ISAIAH 58:13

Continue to write your plan for the upcoming Sabbath.

What personal interests might God be asking you to say no to on that day?

Perhaps activities that drain you, like work?

Running errands?

Preparing for the upcoming week?

Obligatory social events?

Resist the temptation to feel guilty for saying no by reminding yourself that God desires this day to be set apart for resting with Him.

Worry-Free Sabbath

♥

I gave them My Sabbath days of rest as a sign between them and Me.
It was to remind them that I am the LORD, Who had set them apart to be holy.
EZEKIEL 20:12

How can you rest from worry this Sabbath?

Make a list of things that promote stress and anxiety in you, such as checking email, budgeting, making to-do lists for the week, or having a tense conversation.

When you find yourself tempted to engage in one of these things, ask the Lord to help you relax instead.

How might refraining from worrisome activities help you focus better on enjoying the Lord that day?

What Is God Doing on the Sabbath?

Jesus said to them, "The Sabbath was made to meet the needs of people, and not people to meet the requirements of the Sabbath."

MARK 2:27

Scholar Eugene H. Peterson said, "If you don't take a Sabbath, something is wrong. You're doing too much, you're being too much in charge. You've got to quit, one day a week, and just watch what God is doing when you're not doing anything."[14]

Read the above verse again slowly with this quote in mind. Then ask the Lord what need of yours He desires to meet by giving you a Sabbath.

A need for rest?

Worship?

Surrender?

Comfort?

Healing?

End the week by thanking God that He cares enough to meet your needs through the Sabbath.

WEEK 33

Choose to Trust

❤

You are God, O Sovereign LORD. Your words are truth,
and You have promised these good things to Your servant.

2 SAMUEL 7:28

Do you tend to dwell on problems and give in to worry? Many of us spend too much of our time fretting over things we cannot control.

Trusting God, however, means believing that He loves you, that He's absolutely good, and that He wants to do good things in your life. Growing your trust in God begins when you determine the places where it is difficult to trust Him and then choose to let them go into His care.

The exercises this week will help you wrestle with the areas where trust is hard for you. They will encourage you to bring these areas before God, cast your cares on Him, and embrace trusting God one day at a time.

Trusting God is not only a moment-by-moment decision; it is a lifelong process. Go to God as a little child and tell Him your worries and fears. Watch how He transforms your heart when you choose to believe His promise that He has everything under control.

Needing to Trust

Trust in the Lord with all your heart;
do not depend on your own understanding.
Seek His will in all you do, and He will
show you which path to take.

PROVERBS 3:5-6

We learn to trust God when we put ourselves in situations where we *need* to trust Him.

What is something that you deeply desire to trust God with?

The safety and care of your family?

Your finances?

Your job?

A difficult or stressful situation?

Prayerfully ask God how He might be urging you to step out in faith and trust Him today.

Do Not Be Afraid

Be strong and courageous! Do not be afraid and do not panic before them. For the LORD your God will personally go ahead of you. He will neither fail you nor abandon you.

DEUTERONOMY 31:6

What event in the near future are you worried about?

What about that situation is stressing you out?

Take a few moments to imagine God already waiting for you when you get there.

He has gone ahead of you.

Imagine Him saying, "It's okay. I already know what is ahead, and I will be there to help you."

How does this make you feel when you think about getting to that situation?

Hand It Over to God

♥

Seek the Kingdom of God above all else, and live righteously,
and He will give you everything you need. So don't
worry about tomorrow, for tomorrow will bring its
own worries. Today's trouble is enough for today.

MATTHEW 6:33–34

Write down something that currently worries you. Then read
what you wrote.

With the above verse in mind, how do you think God views
this worry?

Tuck the paper in your Bible by today's verse as a way to
symbolize that you are giving that worry over to the Lord for this
day.

What Are You Afraid Of?

♥

You heard me when I cried, "Listen to my pleading! Hear my cry for help!"
Yes, You came when I called; You told me, "Do not fear."

LAMENTATIONS 3:56–57

Most worries result from being afraid of something that may or may not happen.

Fear does more to paralyze you than almost anything else:

It keeps you from joy.

It takes away your peace of mind.

It doesn't allow you to move ahead.

Read the verse again and think about the one thing you are most afraid of.

Listen to God speaking these words to you: *Do not fear. Do not fear.*

How do God's words impact your fears in this moment?

How can you carry these words with you throughout today?

Pour Out Your Heart

♥

My victory and honor come from God alone. He is my refuge,
a rock where no enemy can reach me. O my people, trust in Him
at all times. Pour out your heart to Him, for God is our refuge.

PSALM 62:7-8

Pour out your heart to God about a situation that has consumed,
or will consume, your thoughts.

Write on a piece of paper or type on your computer for several
minutes without stopping and just see what comes out.

Don't try to filter your words; just write continuously.

Then read back your prayers, and end the time by asking God
for guidance, peace, and perspective on this situation.

Empty Worry

— ♥ —

When I am afraid, I will put my trust in You.
PSALM 56:3

Nazi concentration camp survivor Corrie ten Boom stated, "Worry does not empty tomorrow of its sorrows; it empties today of its strength."[15]

Think about a worry that is currently on your mind. Engage your body in prayer by holding out your hands and making fists as you pray about this concern.

When you are done praying, open your hands to symbolize releasing control of this issue to God.

As you finish this week of practicing trust in God, think about the areas where have you made progress.

What aspect has been most difficult for you?

WEEK 34

The Greatest Story

♥

Jesus called out to them, "Come, follow Me,
and I will show you how to fish for people!"

MARK 1:17

Some of Jesus' last words on earth were about witnessing. He said to His disciples, "You will be My witnesses, telling people about Me everywhere—in Jerusalem, throughout Judea, in Samaria, and to the ends of the earth" (Acts 1:8).

To "witness" simply means to tell others about something you have experienced. Your story of how you met and grew to love Jesus is the greatest story you can ever tell.

Most of the exercises this week will encourage you to grow as a witness through prayer, preparation, and practice.

Remember that this week is not about leading others to Christ—although that is always a desired outcome! The two main goals of these exercises are for you to better articulate your own story and to grow in courage to tell it.

What's Your Story?

♥

If someone asks about your hope as a believer, always be ready to explain it.
1 PETER 3:15

We must be familiar with our own stories in order to be ready to explain them to others.

Write down a few sentences about why you have placed your hope in Jesus.

Don't worry about the wording or the order in which everything happened—just write from your heart.

After you've finished, ask yourself whether this was easy or difficult.

If it was especially difficult, then keep working on your story over the next several days until you feel assured that you could confidently share it with someone else.

AUG. 22

What Holds You Back?

❤

One night the Lord spoke to Paul in a vision and told him,
"Don't be afraid! Speak out! Don't be silent! For I am with you."
ACTS 18:9-10

What hinders you from telling others about how you met Jesus
and why you follow Him?

Is it fear of rejection?

Lack of confidence?

Feeling like your story isn't good enough?

Take a few moments to talk to God about this.

Choose one specific word to pray for this week: "Lord, as I
practice witnessing this week, help me to be _____
(brave, unafraid, confident, etc.)."

Never Be Ashamed

♥

God has not given us a spirit of fear and timidity, but of power,
love, and self-discipline. So never be ashamed to tell
others about our Lord.... With the strength God gives you,
be ready to suffer with me for the sake of the Good News.
2 TIMOTHY 1:7-8

Think of someone whom you desperately want to know Jesus. Put their name somewhere you will see it frequently to remind you to pray for them.

How can you intentionally create an opportunity to share the life and love of Jesus with them?

Perhaps by doing something kind for them, telling them you are praying for them, or speaking truth into their life?

Sing of His Faithfulness

♥

I will sing of the LORD's unfailing love forever!
Young and old will hear of Your faithfulness.

PSALM 89:1

Read the verse again. Then reflect on something that God has done in your life recently and write a few sentences to post on social media.

For example, what could you thank God for?

What has He brought you through?

How has He answered your prayers over the past year?

What have you recently learned about who God is?

If you don't use social media, find a way to work your reflections into a conversation today.

Growing in Boldness

♥

[Jesus said,] "I tell you the truth, everyone who acknowledges Me publicly here on earth, the Son of Man will also acknowledge in the presence of God's angels."

LUKE 12:8

The members of the council were amazed when they saw the boldness of Peter and John, for they could see that they were ordinary men with no special training in the Scriptures. They also recognized them as men who had been with Jesus.

ACTS 4:13

Grow in boldness by mentioning in a conversation with an unbelieving friend or acquaintance that you follow Jesus.

This may not be an easy thing to do, but ask the Lord to make you confident as you step out in faith.

Write out these verses above and put them somewhere visible to remind you to be bold with those in your life who don't know Jesus.

AUG. 26

Witness with Your Life

♥

Be careful to live properly among your unbelieving neighbors.
Then even if they accuse you of doing wrong, they will see your honorable
behavior, and they will give honor to God when He judges the world.
1 PETER 2:12

Over the past week, what have you learned about your own story with Jesus?

How have you grown in courage to share your story with others?

End this week by asking the Lord to empower you to fulfill His great commission by continuing to tell others about Him through your words and actions.

WEEK 35

AUG. 27

Letting Go for Something Greater

♥

Everyone who has given up houses or brothers or sisters or
father or mother or children or property, for My sake, will receive
a hundred times as much in return and will inherit eternal life.

MATTHEW 19:29

Sacrifice is not just giving things up; rather, it is a kind of substitution. You give up one thing to obtain something of greater value. You relinquish something you think you need or that makes you feel secure and instead rely on God to provide what He knows you need.

Sometimes God will ask you to give up material possessions, attitudes, comfort, time, desires, or habits so you can better experience them in the context of His plans and presence.

Over the next several days, you will reflect on the sacrifices the Lord may be asking you to make in order to experience the better gifts He wants to give you in return.

It will be hard if you look only at the sacrifice involved. Remind yourself of the flip side of sacrifice and trust that God has something even greater in store for you as you learn to let go.

The Cost of Sacrifice

♥

While Jesus was in the Temple, He watched the rich people dropping their gifts in the collection box. Then a poor widow came by and dropped in two small coins. "I tell you the truth," Jesus said, "this poor widow has given more than all the rest of them. For they have given a tiny part of their surplus, but she, poor as she is, has given everything she has."

LUKE 21:1–4

True sacrifice costs something.

Take a moment to pray over what the Lord may be asking you to sacrificially give away this week.

It may not be money or material possessions.

It may be time that you had planned to enjoy working on a hobby.

It may be a habit.

How might this stretch you to rely on God?

A Sacrifice of Praise

♥

Let us offer through Jesus a continual sacrifice of
praise to God, proclaiming our allegiance to His name.
HEBREWS 13:15

Sometimes a continual sacrifice of praise requires us to give up
attitudes that hinder or distract us from thanking God.

What would it mean for you to offer "a continual sacrifice of
praise to God" today?

What feelings or attitudes might God be asking you to give up
so that you can better praise Him?

Anger?

Resentment?

Bitterness?

Self-pity?

Vow to let go of those attitudes for today. If you find yourself
engaging in them, use it as a reminder to praise God instead.

The Sacrifice to Make after Sin

❤

The sacrifice you desire is a broken spirit.
You will not reject a broken and repentant heart, O God.
PSALM 51:17

King David wrote this psalm after he committed adultery with Bathsheba and arranged for her husband's murder. David is saying that the only sacrifice one can offer to God after sinning is a broken, repentant spirit. You sacrifice your pride, and in return God gives you His mercy and forgiveness, which leads to a restored relationship with Him. Your sacrifice is always less than what God gives in return.

Are you able to sacrifice your pride, rationalizations, and excuses, or do you try to make other "sacrifices" to appease Him? For example, do you read your Bible after you explode with anger, or give to the church after spending money on something that doesn't honor God? These activities may help us refocus our hearts, but we must never use them to simply assuage any guilt we may feel.

A Sacrifice of Thanks

♥

Let us come to Him with thanksgiving. Let us sing psalms of
praise to Him. For the Lord is a great God, a great King above all gods.
PSALM 95:2-3

I will offer you a sacrifice of thanksgiving
and call on the name of the Lord.
PSALM 116:17

Sometimes thanking God for our trials feels like a sacrifice.

Perhaps that is because it is hard to let go of feelings of anger,
resentment, or entitlement that have become a comfortable habit.

For what difficult situation can you offer a sacrifice of thanksgiving to God?

If it feels too difficult to thank God for your trials right now, try
instead to thank Him simply for who He is.

Sacrifice for God's Word

♥

I plead with you to give your bodies to God
because of all He has done for you. Let them be a living
and holy sacrifice—the kind He will find acceptable.
ROMANS 12:1

While you are reading this devotional, you are sacrificing a certain amount of time in order to engage with it. You are disciplining your body and mind to give up something else in order to do this.

Sacrifice five more minutes of your time right now by opening your Bible to Psalm 28 and enjoying the Lord and His Word.

Offering Moments to God

♥

As for me, my life has already been poured out as an offering to God.
2 TIMOTHY 4:6

Practice offering your life to God today by sacrificing the need for immediate gratification.

As you go through the day, be aware of when you want to satisfy an impulse, such as a craving for chocolate, the urge to turn on the TV, or a desire to check your social media. Then spend a minute to sacrifice that desire or impulse to the Lord.

See if He has something better in mind for you, or just enjoy an extra minute in His presence. Expect Him to speak to your heart.

As you conclude these days of practicing sacrifice, when has God graciously allowed you to experience blessing from sacrifice this past week?

WEEK 36

SEP. 3

Lead with the Body

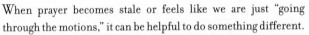

Pray like this ...
MATTHEW 6:9

When prayer becomes stale or feels like we are just "going through the motions," it can be helpful to do something different.

One way to do this is to use our bodies during prayer. Different postures help us physically express the attitudes of our hearts to God.

The postures in the exercises over the next week will use your body to move your heart toward a place of humility, boldness, submission, gratitude, reverence, and worship.

Communication with God does not require a certain physical position, and God won't be more likely to answer your prayers because you are on your knees rather than sitting. But remember that the body and heart are very much connected. Often when you lead with the body, the heart will follow.

This week's exercises may feel unnatural for you. Lean into the discomfort and be honest with God about what you feel as you engage in these exercises. Ask God to open the posture of your heart as you use your body in prayer.

SEP. 4

Face Down

♥

Moses and Aaron turned away from the people and went to the
entrance of the Tabernacle, where they fell face down on the ground.
Then the glorious presence of the LORD appeared to them.

NUMBERS 20:6

Lying down before the Lord with our faces toward the ground puts
our hearts in a posture of humility.

Begin today prostrate before God, confessing your tendency
toward sin and recognizing the depth of your need for His mercy,
forgiveness, and provision.

Realize your inadequacy and your inability to live this day
apart from Him.

If there is a certain crisis in your life, acknowledge that God is
the only one who can deliver you.

Stand Up

♥

Solomon stood before the altar of the LORD in front of the entire community of Israel. He lifted his hands toward heaven, and he prayed.

1 KINGS 8:22–23

Standing before a king means that you have been legally justified to be in his presence.

When you stand in prayer, it reflects confidence in your place of undeserved privilege before God because of Christ (see Romans 5:2).

Stand boldly before God in prayer today.

Thank Him that you can stand before Him clothed in righteousness because of what Christ has done.

End the prayer by telling Him what you are confidently and joyfully looking forward to in eternity with Him.

Sit Down

♥

King David went in and sat before the LORD and prayed.
2 SAMUEL 7:18

In Scripture, sitting signifies having a permanent relationship with God and enjoying His presence.

When you sit before God, you acknowledge your place of belonging in His family. Christ has saved you a seat next to Him in heaven at the banquet table because you have been adopted by God (see Ephesians 2:6).

Sit with God in prayer today.

Thank Him for adopting you as His own and giving you a place of permanent belonging.

Continue on in prayer, imagining what it will feel like to sit with Jesus at His table in heaven.

Kneel before Him

♥

When Solomon finished making these prayers and petitions to
the LORD, he stood up in front of the altar of the LORD, where
he had been kneeling with his hands raised toward heaven.

1 KINGS 8:54

King Solomon knelt before God and prayed for the Temple and
the entire congregation of Israel.

When you ask God for help, kneeling before Him puts your
heart in an attitude of submission.

Kneeling signifies that no matter how He chooses to answer
your prayers, you can trust that it is the best thing for you.

Kneel before the Lord today and begin your prayer by ac-
knowledging that He is Lord of all the earth.

Present your requests to Him and end your prayer by asking
that His will be done.

Look Up

♥

They rolled the stone aside. Then Jesus looked up to
heaven and said, "Father, thank You for hearing me."

JOHN 11:41

The Bible mentions several times that Jesus looked up to heaven
and prayed.

When you look someone in the face, it shows that you have an
intimate relationship with them. You trust that person enough to
be honest and open with them.

Lift your face to God in prayer today.

Acknowledge that He is your trusted helper, friend, and confidant.

Tell Him about something on your heart that you would say
only to a very close friend.

Raise Your Hands

Lift your hands toward the sanctuary, and praise the LORD.
May the LORD, Who made heaven and earth, bless you from Jerusalem.
PSALM 134:2-3

Raising your hands in prayer symbolizes seeking God's mercy and blessing.

When you raise your hands, you reflect a readiness to receive all God has for you today, and you remember all His provisions in the past.

Raise your hands to God in prayer.

Thank Him specifically for how He blessed you yesterday, and humbly ask Him to help you see His blessings today.

WEEK 37

SEP. 10

Step Away and Take a Pause

♥

The LORD is my shepherd; I have all that I need.
He lets me rest in green meadows; He leads me beside
peaceful streams. He renews my strength. He guides me.
PSALM 23:1-3

We live, in fact, in a world starved for solitude, silence, and privacy, and therefore starved for meditation and true friendship," wrote C. S. Lewis.[16]

Solitude involves intentionally stepping away from normal human interaction in order to grow in friendship with the Lord. We do not enter solitude to *do* things for God; we enter solitude to simply *be* with God. Solitude helps us pause regularly from work, endless activity, and overwhelming obligations to focus on God. Many of us avoid and even fear being alone—perhaps because without our distractions and defenses, we are left to face ourselves in the light of God's truth.

As you practice solitude this week, you may experience feelings of confusion, distraction, irrational fear, emptiness, or even condemnation. If this happens, acknowledge these feelings before God and remember His promise to always be with you.

Just Be with Me

Before daybreak the next morning, Jesus got
up and went out to an isolated place to pray.

MARK 1:35

What small spaces of alone time are already incorporated into
your day—time spent showering? Driving? Exercising? Mowing
the lawn? Cooking?

Choose one of those times to dedicate to being alone with
God. Before you do this, turn off any additional noise that may
compete for your attention.

Don't try to make anything happen; simply use the time and
space to focus on being in God's presence and to talk to Him about
whatever comes to mind.

Step Back to Draw Close

Immediately after this, Jesus insisted that His disciples
get back into the boat and head across the lake to Bethsaida,
while He sent the people home. After telling everyone
good-bye, He went up into the hills by Himself to pray.

MARK 6:45-46

Read the verses and think about what it might have been like for Jesus to send away His disciples in order to be alone.

Which relationships are difficult to step back from in order to spend time alone with God?

In the next few minutes of solitude, acknowledge this tension in prayer and then offer that person or those people to the Lord, trusting they are in His care.

A Walk with God

♥

When the cool evening breezes were blowing, the man and
his wife heard the LORD God walking about in the garden. So they
hid from the LORD God among the trees. Then the LORD God
called to the man, "Where are you?" He replied, "I heard You
walking in the garden, so I hid. I was afraid because I was naked."

GENESIS 3:8-10

Adam and Eve recognized the sound of God walking in the garden. Perhaps the evening was their special time to walk and talk
together.

Schedule a time to take a walk alone with the Lord today—even
if the walk is only five minutes.

Picture Him being beside you.

Resist the urge to fill the time with any sounds or words, and
just enjoy being in God's company.

The Role of Solitude in Decisions

❤

*One day soon afterward Jesus went up on a mountain to pray,
and He prayed to God all night. At daybreak He called together
all of His disciples and chose twelve of them to be apostles.*

LUKE 6:12–13

Jesus made one of the most important decisions of His ministry—choosing His disciples—after He spent time alone praying to God.

What big decision or transition is coming up in your life?

Is it a financial decision?

Deciding whether or not to continue a ministry?

A difficult choice involving your children?

Schedule a time on your calendar right now to spend an extended amount of time with God before you need to finalize this upcoming decision.

Sitting in Silence with God

The LORD is good to those who depend on Him, to those who search for Him. So it is good to wait quietly for salvation from the LORD.... Let them sit alone in silence beneath the LORD's demands.

LAMENTATIONS 3:25-26, 28

What do you usually do when you spend time alone with God?

Do you pray? Read your Bible? Journal?

As good as these activities are, sometimes they can distract you from simply being with God.

Let go of "doing" and "producing" in your time with God today. Don't try to make something happen—just be yourself with the One who created you.

Sit in silence with God for at least five minutes.

Begin by praying, "Lord, I just want to be with You." If distracting thoughts come to mind, jot them down to deal with another time.

Your Special Place with God

Accompanied by the disciples, Jesus left the
upstairs room and went as usual to the Mount of Olives.
LUKE 22:39

The Mount of Olives was a sacred space that Jesus shared with God the Father.

Where are the special places of companionship between just you and God?

If you haven't had such a place, think of somewhere you'd like to declare as your private space with Him.

Perhaps you could choose a favorite room in your home, a beautiful spot in nature, or the corner of a coffee shop. (If you are having difficulty deciding on a location, think about where you have felt closest to God in the past.)

Make it a habit to go to your special place regularly to spend time with the Lord.

WEEK 38

SEP. 17

The Anchor of the Soul

♥

> O Lord, You alone are my hope.
> **PSALM 71:5**

There is a universal expectation for good in this life—even in the midst of adversity. The need or desire to trust that things will get better is what the concept of *hope* is all about.

When you long for life to get better, where do you place your hope—in your own abilities, good fortune, or help from others? Or does your hope come from trusting God? Only when you trust God with your future can true hope begin to grow, because He created you with a great future in mind.

This week you will practice hoping in God, not just experiencing hope itself. This will require addressing where your current hope lies and choosing instead to hope in God. Hope in God gives you confident joy in the face of uncertainty because it anchors your soul and future to Him (see Hebrews 6:19).

Begin this week by being honest with God about your hopes. Many of these exercises involve meditating on God's wonderful promises in His Word and allowing these truths to grow your hope in Him alone.

What Do You Hope For?

♥

Lord, where do I put my hope? My only hope is in You.

PSALM 39:7

How would you finish this statement: "I am hoping for …"?

Are you hoping for a new job?

A new relationship?

A life change?

How would your happiness be affected if what you hoped for didn't happen?

Ask God what it would be like to let go of this hope.

How would this open you to your need for Him?

Hope from God's Word

♥

Such things were written in the Scriptures long ago to teach us.
And the Scriptures give us hope and encouragement
as we wait patiently for God's promises to be fulfilled.

ROMANS 15:4

Read the introduction to this week one more time.

Then choose a Scripture that encourages you to place your hope in God.

Write it down and post it somewhere visible this week. (Suggestions: Romans 8:28; Lamentations 3:22-23; 2 Corinthians 5:17; Jeremiah 29:11.)

In Whom Is Your Confidence?

♥

Don't put your confidence in powerful people; there is no help for you there. When they breathe their last, they return to the earth, and all their plans die with them. But joyful are those who have the God of Israel as their helper, whose hope is in the LORD their God.

PSALM 146:3–5

Are there certain people you have come to rely on more than God?

What qualities do they possess that make you trust them?

Do you have trouble believing that God possesses those same trustworthy characteristics? Why?

Remember that God loves you and desires an authentic relationship with you, so take time to talk honestly with Him about what keeps you from fully trusting Him.

Looking Back for Future Hope

Now all glory to God, Who is able, through His mighty
power at work within us, to accomplish infinitely more than
we might ask or think. Glory to Him in the church and in
Christ Jesus through all generations forever and ever! Amen.

EPHESIANS 3:20-21

Write down a hope you have for the future.

Now think back to a time when God did something that exceeded
anything you could have ever hoped for.

Write a prayer underneath your future hope, asking God to
help you place your hope in Him rather than in your own plans.

This could be the start of a prayer journal to encourage you in
difficult times.

Where Hope Is Most Needed

❤

Let us hold tightly without wavering to the hope
we affirm, for God can be trusted to keep His promise.
HEBREWS 10:23

Read through God's promises listed below and ask yourself which
of them you need to hold most tightly to today.

- God's promise to be with you (see Deuteronomy 31:6)
- God's promise to always love you (see Romans 8:38)
- God's promise to always be ready to help in times of
  distress (see Psalm 46:1)
- God's promise to fulfill good plans for your life
  (see Jeremiah 29:11)
- God's promise to secure your eternal salvation
  (see 1 John 4:9-10)

Once you have chosen a verse, read it aloud several times until
it really sinks in. Think of a situation that is heavy on your heart.
With this in mind, ask God to help you hold tightly to the promise
you just read.

Expect Great Things

I am trusting You, O LORD, saying, "You are my God!"
My future is in Your hands.... How great is the
goodness You have stored up for those who fear You.
PSALM 31:14-15, 19

Read the verses again with your own future in mind.

Remind yourself not simply to desire good things for your future, but to *expect* great things for your future—because that's what God has promised you.

As you end this week of practicing "hope in God," thank Him for having your future in His hands and for the great things He has in store for you.

WEEK 39

Wait and Watch

❤

As for me, I look to the LORD for help. I wait confidently
for God to save me, and my God will certainly hear me.
MICAH 7:7

We are all waiting for something—a different job, a restored relationship (or a new one), physical healing, a loved one to come home, or things just to get better.

Each of us has prayers that remain unanswered. Seasons of waiting can seem like a waste of time, but what if waiting is actually a gift?

The practice of "waiting well" is making the most of the time at hand. The only way to grow into a person who "waits well" is through experience—in other words, through a lot of waiting!

The next week focuses on learning from our seasons of waiting to be more hopeful in God's plan for us, to be more persistent in prayer, to be more confident and courageous as we wait, and to resist the urge to rush ahead of God's timing.

No matter how difficult or pointless waiting feels, trust that God will use your waiting as a gift of time, not a waste of it.

Growing Your Hope

♥

Let all that I am wait quietly before God, for my hope is in Him. He alone is my rock and my salvation, my fortress where I will not be shaken.

PSALM 62:5-6

Choose one thing you are currently waiting on the Lord for. Think back to last week's practice of hope and reflect on where you put your hope as you wait.

Do you place your hope in believing it will all work out?

In anticipation that God will answer your prayer in the way you would like Him to?

Or in confidence that God is already at work carrying out the plan He knows is best for you?

What would it look like to hope only in God as you wait, knowing that He is preparing you for what lies ahead?

Growing Your Service

♥

Be still before the LORD and wait patiently for Him; do not fret when people succeed in their ways, when they carry out their wicked schemes.

PSALM 37:7, NIV

Hymn writer P. Doddridge wrote, "Blest are the humble souls, that wait with sweet submission to His will; harmonious all their passions move, and in the midst of storms are still."[17]

As you wait for God to do His work in situations you can't control, don't be idle.

Serve Him where you are, doing the little things right.

Ask God how He might want you to use your times of waiting. Does He want you to be still?

To rejoice?

To read His Word?

To pray?

To serve someone else?

Growing Your Patience

Better to be patient than powerful; better
to have self-control than to conquer a city.
PROVERBS 16:32

Practice patience by intentionally putting yourself in a place where you need to wait a little longer.

For example, choose the longest checkout line at the store, drive in the slow lane, or make a recipe that takes longer to cook.

While you are waiting, reflect about what is going on inside your heart.

Are you anxious? Tense? Angry?

Use the time to talk to the Lord about what it feels like for you to wait.

Growing Your Perspective

———— ♥ ————

[God said,] "I will send terror ahead of you to drive out the Hivites, Canaanites, and Hittites. But I will not drive them out in a single year, because the land would become desolate and the wild animals would multiply and threaten you. I will drive them out a little at a time until your population has increased enough to take possession of the land."

EXODUS 23:28–30

———————————————

God's decision to slowly drive out the Hivites, Canaanites, and Hittites was actually for the Israelites' good so He could protect them and ultimately provide more abundantly for them.

Was there ever a time when God didn't fully answer your prayer right away?

As you look back, what blessings came during that time of waiting?

What are you waiting for now?

How might your wait yield far better results than if you got what you asked for now?

Growing Your Soul

❤

She called Mary aside from the mourners and told her, "The Teacher
is here and wants to see you." So Mary immediately went to Him....
When Mary arrived and saw Jesus, she fell at his feet and said,
"Lord, if only You had been here, my brother would not have died."
JOHN 11:28–29, 32

Read this passage again. Imagine you are Mary and it is your own
brother who has died.

You have been waiting for Jesus to help your brother, and now
Jesus has finally arrived four days after his death.

When Jesus asks to speak with you, what do you want to say to
Him?

How does your response reveal how your heart handles seasons of waiting?

Growing Your Confidence

♥

I am confident I will see the Lord's goodness while I am
here in the land of the living. Wait patiently for the Lord.
Be brave and courageous. Yes, wait patiently for the Lord.
PSALM 27:13-14

Rejoice in our confident hope. Be patient
in trouble, and keep on praying.
ROMANS 12:12

Make a list of things you have waited for that God eventually provided.

Now make another list of things you are currently waiting on God for.

How do answered prayers from the past encourage you to wait with patience and confidence in the present?

WEEK 40

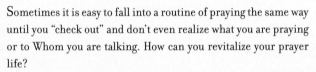

Enter into God's Story

♥

Then Jesus told this story …
LUKE 13:6

Sometimes it is easy to fall into a routine of praying the same way until you "check out" and don't even realize what you are praying or to Whom you are talking. How can you revitalize your prayer life?

Your imagination can be a powerful tool to help you engage with God in a new way. Imaginative prayer is an active way of praying that engages your mind and heart as you imagine yourself in a scene from Scripture. In his book *Prayer*, Richard Foster writes, "We begin to enter the story and make it our own. We move from detached observation to active participation."[18]

This week you will practice entering into Scripture with Jesus as you watch the story evolve. The instructions are the same for each day: Read the passage once, and then read it again—this time imagining yourself in the story.

Remember that your imagination is a gift from God. Ask the Holy Spirit to use this gift to deepen your relationship with Jesus as you experience Him through His Word.

Blind Bartimaeus

♥

Bartimaeus … began to shout, "Jesus, Son of David,
have mercy on me!" "Be quiet!" many of the people yelled
at him. But he only shouted louder, "Son of David, have mercy
on me!" When Jesus heard him, He stopped and said,
"Tell him to come here." So they called the blind man.
"Cheer up," they said. "Come on, He's calling you!" Bartimaeus
threw aside his coat, jumped up, and came to Jesus.
"What do you want Me to do for you?" Jesus asked.

MARK 10:47–51

Imagine yourself in the scene.

- Who are you? A main character or a bystander?
- Engage your senses. What do you see, smell, hear, taste, and feel?
- What emotions rise up as you imagine yourself in this scene?
- What do you want to say to Jesus in response to His question? Make this your prayer for today.

The Woman Who Couldn't Stop Bleeding

❤

A woman who had suffered for twelve years with constant bleeding
came up behind him. She touched the fringe of His robe, for she thought,
"If I can just touch His robe, I will be healed." Jesus turned around,
and when He saw her He said, "Daughter, be encouraged! Your faith
has made you well." And the woman was healed at that moment.

MATTHEW 9:20-22

Imagine yourself in the scene.

- Who are you? A main character or a bystander?
- Engage your senses. What do you see, smell, hear, taste, and feel?
- What emotions rise up as you imagine yourself in this scene?
- What do you want to say to Jesus? Make this your prayer for today.

The Sick Man by the Pool

♥

Inside the city, near the Sheep Gate, was the pool of Bethesda....
One of the men lying there had been sick for thirtyeight years. [Jesus] …
asked him, "Would you like to get well?" "I can't, Sir," the sick man said,
"for I have no one to put me into the pool when the water bubbles up.
Someone else always gets there ahead of me." Jesus told him,
"Stand up, pick up your mat, and walk!" Instantly, the man was healed!

JOHN 5:2, 5–9

Imagine yourself in the scene.

- Who are you? A main character or a bystander?
- Engage your senses. What do you see, smell, hear, taste, and feel?
- What emotions rise up as you imagine yourself in this scene?
- What do you want to say to Jesus? Make this your prayer for today.

OCT. 5

Jesus Quiets a Storm

♥

Jesus got into the boat and started across the lake with His disciples.
Suddenly, a fierce storm struck the lake, with waves breaking into the boat.
But Jesus was sleeping. The disciples went and woke Him up, shouting,
"Lord, save us! We're going to drown!" Jesus responded, "Why are you
afraid? You have so little faith!" Then He got up and rebuked the wind and
waves, and suddenly there was a great calm. The disciples were amazed.
"Who is this man?" they asked. "Even the winds and waves obey Him!"

MATTHEW 8:23-27

Imagine yourself in the scene.

- Who are you? A main character or a bystander?
- Engage your senses. What do you see, smell, hear, taste, and feel?
- What emotions rise up as you imagine yourself in this scene?
- What do you want to say to Jesus? Make this your prayer for today.

Jesus Dies on the Cross

❤

Jesus shouted, "Father, I entrust My spirit into Your hands!"
And with those words He breathed His last. When the Roman officer
overseeing the execution saw what had happened, he worshiped
God and said, "Surely this man was innocent." And when all the crowd
that came to see the crucifixion saw what had happened, they went
home in deep sorrow. But Jesus' friends, including the women
who had followed Him from Galilee, stood at a distance watching.

LUKE 23:46–49

Imagine yourself in the scene.

- Who are you? A main character or a bystander?
- Engage your senses. What do you see, smell, hear, taste, and feel?
- What emotions rise up as you imagine yourself in this scene?
- What do you want to say to Jesus? Make this your prayer for today.

Jesus Appears to His Disciples

♥

The two from Emmaus told their story of how Jesus had appeared to them.... And just as they were telling about it, Jesus Himself was suddenly standing there among them. "Peace be with you," He said. But the whole group was startled and frightened, thinking they were seeing a ghost! "Why are you frightened?" He asked. "Why are your hearts filled with doubt?"

LUKE 24:35-38

Imagine yourself in the scene.

- Who are you? A main character or a bystander?
- Engage your senses. What do you see, smell, hear, taste, and feel?
- What emotions rise up as you imagine yourself in this scene?
- What do you want to say to Jesus? Make this your prayer for today.
- How have the last several days of practicing imaginative prayer changed your perspective on praying?

WEEK 41

OCT. 8

Can You Keep a Secret?

♥

When you pray, go away by yourself, shut the door
behind you, and pray to your Father in private.
Then your Father, who sees everything, will reward you.

MATTHEW 6:6

Have you ever done something really kind for someone else and then wanted to slip it into a conversation with others? The practice of "secrecy" is keeping certain things just between you and God. Secrets are usually seen as bad, and sometimes they are. There are many places in Scripture, however, where the ability to keep a secret is an important character trait. Jesus asked those He healed to keep their interactions with Him a secret. He spoke of the importance of keeping some prayers and good deeds secret in order to keep one's motives pure.

This week, you will practice secrecy in three different ways: first, by abstaining from telling others about your good deeds in order to deny yourself attention from them; second, by intentionally keeping the secrets of others in order to strengthen your trustworthiness; and third, by developing secrets with the Lord as a way to deepen your relationship with Him.

Give Anonymously

♥

When you give to someone in need, don't let your left hand
know what your right hand is doing. Give your gifts in
private, and your Father, who sees everything, will reward you.

MATTHEW 6:3-4

Give to someone anonymously today.

For instance, pay for the person behind you at the drive-
through, leave an encouraging note on a windshield, drop off a
small gift on someone's desk or doorstep, or donate to a charity
without telling anyone.

How does it feel to give gifts in secret?

Read the verse above again and ask yourself this question: "Is
God's reward enough for me?"

Giving Motives

♥

When you give to someone in need, don't do as the
hypocrites do—blowing trumpets in the synagogues and
streets to call attention to their acts of charity! I tell you
the truth, they have received all the reward they will ever get.

MATTHEW 6:2

Spend a few minutes with God reflecting on these questions:

- Do you give so others can see how "spiritual" you are?
- Do you mention your gifts or volunteer work in conversation to receive praise?
- When you give, are you more focused on what others think about your gifts than on simply pleasing God?
- Do you feel hurt, rejected, or disappointed when someone does not respond the way you want over a gift you have given them?

If you answered yes to any of these questions, what can you do today to begin to change your attitude?

Prayer Motives

♥

When you pray, don't be like the hypocrites who love to pray
publicly on street corners and in the synagogues where everyone can
see them. I tell you the truth, that is all the reward they will ever get.

MATTHEW 6:5

Spend a few minutes reflecting with God on the following questions:

• Do you pray or mention prayer in conversation so people can
see how "spiritual" you are?
• When you pray with others, are you more focused on what they
think or on simply pleasing God?
• Do you try to sound more intelligent, religious, or passionate
when you pray publicly than when you pray alone?

As you did yesterday, if you answered yes to any of these
questions, what can you intentionally do today to begin to change
your attitude?

Only God Knows

♥

Instantly the leprosy disappeared, and the man was healed. Then Jesus
sent him on his way with a stern warning: "Don't tell anyone about this.
Instead, go to the priest and let him examine you. Take along the
offering required in the law of Moses for those who have been healed of
leprosy. This will be a public testimony that you have been cleansed."

MARK 1:42–44

What secrets exist just between you and God?

Do you have a secret place you share together?

A favorite memory that only you and God know about?

A meaningful time of confession where you felt His grace and
forgiveness?

Spend some time reflecting on how these secret moments
impact your intimacy with God.

What secret can you share with God today that you have told
no one else?

A Trustworthy Confidence

♥

A gossip goes around telling secrets,
but those who are trustworthy can keep a confidence.
PROVERBS 11:13

When arguing with your neighbor, don't betray another
person's secret. Others may accuse you of gossip,
and you will never regain your good reputation.
PROVERBS 25:9-10

Make a commitment before the Lord that you will keep the secrets others have entrusted to you.

Ask Him to prompt your conscience when you are tempted to share secrets.

Pray right now for strength to control your tongue so you can be a trustworthy confidant.

Bragging Rights

———— ♥ ————

Don't be selfish; don't try to impress others.
Be humble, thinking of others as better than yourselves.

PHILIPPIANS 2:3

What situations or people most tempt you to brag about your actions, achievements, or talents?

What is your motive for doing this?

Is it to feel like you measure up?

To gain approval?

To feel better about yourself?

Take a few moments to confess this to God.

End these exercises on secrecy by telling God about a need you have. Don't tell anyone else about it.

Write down this secret need so that when God decides to meet it, you will know it was because of Him and not someone else.

WEEK 42

OCT. 15

Open Your Home and Your Heart

♥

Don't forget to show hospitality to strangers, for some who
have done this have entertained angels without realizing it!

HEBREWS 13:2

Many people avoid hospitality because they feel that their homes or cooking skills are inadequate. Some may find it difficult to share their time, space, and resources. Jesus didn't have a home, yet He was constantly welcoming people into His presence.

We are called to do likewise with the resources we have—to graciously receive others into our homes, feed them, and make them feel welcome. Hospitality is about becoming a safe person and cultivating a safe space in which others can experience the welcoming presence of God. It is a way to obey and serve God, because God calls us to love and serve others as though we are serving Him.

This week, set aside your own expectations and insecurities in order to practice hospitality. Don't just open your home to entertain others—embrace them fully by giving them your presence and sharing your life with them. Remember that it is your presence, not your presentation, that makes others feel welcome.

Put Out the Welcome Mat

♥

Cheerfully share your home with those
who need a meal or a place to stay.
1 PETER 4:9

How can you "cheerfully" practice hospitality this week?

Can you cook dinner for someone without complaining?

Open your home without fretting over the mess?

Graciously allow others into your space?

Thank God for your friends and your home as you prepare for
their arrival?

Ask God whom He would like you to invite over.

Call, text, or email that person today to set up a time to have
them over for a meal, a cup of coffee, or dessert.

Prayer Preparation

♥

As soon as they arrived, they prayed for these new believers.
ACTS 8:15

The people of the island were very kind to us. It was cold
and rainy, so they built a fire on the shore to welcome us.
ACTS 28:2

There are many things we can do to welcome others into our homes. But one thing we often forget to do as we prepare for others is to pray.

Get in the practice of praying for others before they arrive at your home.

Think through the week ahead and pray for those who may come through your doors, such as family members, neighbors, out-of-town visitors, or people doing work on your home.

Write down their names and spend a few moments praying that each person who enters your home will feel peace and the welcoming presence of Jesus through you.

A Place in Your Father's House

♥

[Jesus said,] "Don't let your hearts be troubled. Trust in God, and trust also in Me. There is more than enough room in My Father's home. If this were not so, would I have told you that I am going to prepare a place for you?"
JOHN 14:1-2

Hospitality is close to God's heart—so much so that He has promised to prepare a room especially for you.

Close your eyes and imagine walking into the room Jesus has prepared just for you in His heavenly home.

How do you picture it?

What details has God included that He knew you would like?

What kind of host is God?

As you consider how God prepares for you, what special thing can you prepare to let your guests know you were looking forward to hosting them?

Feeling Welcomed

♥

May the Lord show special kindness to Onesiphorus and
all his family because he often visited and encouraged me.
He was never ashamed of me because I was in chains.

2 TIMOTHY 1:16

Author Jen Wilkin describes the difference between entertaining and hospitality by stating, "Entertaining seeks to *impress*. Hospitality seeks to *bless*."[19]

How often do you try to impress others rather than bless them?

Ask a few close friends how they felt in your presence the first time they were invited into your home.

Did they feel welcomed and safe?

Did you try to get to know them by asking thoughtful questions?

Did you give them your full attention when you were together?

Be open and receptive to their answers. Set aside any defensiveness; simply listen and be open.

Golden Rule Hospitality

♥

Do to others whatever you would like them to do to you.
This is the essence of all that is taught in the law and the prophets.

MATTHEW 7:12

When have you been blessed by the hospitality of another? Think about what specifically blessed you.

Was it the food and drink? An atmosphere of warmth? A listening ear? Good conversation and thoughtful questions? Your host's undivided attention?

How can you follow the Golden Rule and serve others as you would like to be served?

Write out a short mission statement for you and your family of how you would like to treat those who come into your home.

For example, your statement could be "It is the goal of our family to create a safe and nurturing space for our guests by feeding them good food, asking them good questions, and being good listeners."

Routine Welcome

♥

When God's people are in need, be ready to help them.
Always be eager to practice hospitality.

ROMANS 12:13

What are some ways you can welcome someone into your every-day routine?

Perhaps you could invite someone to join you on errands or as you pick up your kids from school. Or you could offer to help someone cook a meal or get ready for an event.

As you come to the end of this week of practicing hospitality, in what specific area have you felt most convicted?

Ask God for the commitment and perseverance to continue your spiritual exercises in that area.

WEEK 43

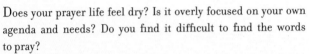

A Powerful Way to Pray

Revive me by Your word.

PSALM 119:25

Does your prayer life feel dry? Is it overly focused on your own agenda and needs? Do you find it difficult to find the words to pray?

Praying Scripture is a powerful practice that uses the Bible as fresh language for prayer. When you don't even know how to begin to pray, the book of Psalms is a great place to start.

This week, begin each morning by taking a few moments to be silent before the Lord and then reading the day's psalm out loud as a prayer. As you pray the honest, heartfelt prayer of someone who lived thousands of years ago, think about how the words relate to your life.

The reflection questions after each psalm can help you continue the conversation with God. If your prayers still feel dry, short, or too simple, that's okay!

Trust God to listen and to honor even the messiest and most imperfect prayers. Allow yourself to simply rest in God's presence, confident that He knows and cares about everything on your heart.

Show Me Where to Walk

❤

I lift my hands to You in prayer. I thirst for You as parched land thirsts
for rain. Come quickly, LORD, and answer me, for my depression
deepens. Don't turn away from me, or I will die. Let me hear of
Your unfailing love each morning, for I am trusting You. Show me
where to walk, for I give myself to You. Rescue me from my enemies,
LORD; I run to You to hide me. Teach me to do Your will, for You are
my God. May Your gracious Spirit lead me forward on a firm footing.

PSALM 143:6–10

As you pray through this psalm, choose a word or phrase that
most resonates with your heart.

Spend a few minutes talking to God about what in your life
caused you to choose this word.

Finish by praying through this Scripture one more time.

Create in Me a Clean Heart

Have mercy on me, O God, because of Your unfailing love.
Because of Your great compassion, blot out the stain of my sins.
Wash me clean from my guilt. Purify me from my sin.... For I was born a
sinner—yes, from the moment my mother conceived me. But You desire
honesty from the womb, teaching me wisdom even there. Purify me from
my sins, and I will be clean; wash me, and I will be whiter than snow.
Oh, give me back my joy again; You have broken me—now let me rejoice....
Create in me a clean heart, O God. Renew a loyal spirit within me....
Restore to me the joy of your salvation, and make me willing to obey You.

PSALM 51:1-2, 5-8, 10, 12

What do you need to confess to God? Continue in prayer, using
these verses as a guide.

You Are My Safe Refuge

♥

O God, listen to my cry! Hear my prayer! From the ends of
the earth, I cry to You for help when my heart is overwhelmed.
Lead me to the towering rock of safety, for You are my safe refuge,
a fortress where my enemies cannot reach me. Let me live
forever in Your sanctuary, safe beneath the shelter of Your wings!

PSALM 61:1-4

Talk to God about what is overwhelming you. Then read this passage again with your burdens in mind.

End this time by thanking God for being "a towering rock of safety" and a "safe refuge."

Hear Me As I Pray

❤

O LORD, hear me as I pray; pay attention to my groaning. Listen to my
cry for help, my King and my God, for I pray to no one but You. Listen
to my voice in the morning, LORD. Each morning I bring my requests
to You and wait expectantly.... Lead me in the right path, O LORD....
Make Your way plain for me to follow.... [L]et all who take refuge
in You rejoice; let them sing joyful praises forever. Spread Your
protection over them, that all who love Your name may be filled with joy.

PSALM 5:1-3, 8, 11

Continue in prayer by bringing specific requests to God and
asking Him to help you wait expectantly for His answers and His
timing.

Your Hope Is in God

———— ♥ ————

"LORD, remind me how brief my time on earth will be.
Remind me that my days are numbered—how fleeting my life is.
You have made my life no longer than the width of my hand.
My entire lifetime is just a moment to You; at best, each of us
is but a breath." … And so, Lord, where do I put my hope?
My only hope is in You…. Hear my prayer, O LORD!
Listen to my cries for help! Don't ignore my tears.
For I am Your guest—a traveler passing through…. I cry out
to God Most High, to God who will fulfill His purpose for me.
PSALM 39:4-5, 7, 12; PSALM 57:2

Talk with God about the brevity of life and how you desire this
knowledge to impact what you do and say every day.

Rejoice in the Lord

♥

Let all that I am praise the LORD. O LORD my God, how great You are!
You are robed with honor and majesty.... O LORD, what a variety of
things You have made! In wisdom You have made them all. The earth
is full of Your creatures.... When You give them Your breath, life
is created, and You renew the face of the earth.... I will sing to
the LORD as long as I live. I will praise my God to my last breath!

PSALM 104:1, 24, 30, 33

Thank God for His beautiful and amazing creation, for your life,
and for the lives of your loved ones.

Praise Him, marveling at the fact that the God of the universe
chose to create you and wants to have a relationship with you.

WEEK 44

Freedom from Indulgence

❤

No one can serve two masters. For you will hate one and love
the other; you will be devoted to one and despise the other.
You cannot serve God and be enslaved to money.

LUKE 16:13

Almost everyone has heard the phrase "Money is power." Whether
we live in wealth or poverty, money has the power to replace God
as master of our lives.

Frugality means choosing to spend less money on our own
pleasure, prestige, and comfort. It is living below our means to be
free from wants (and debts!) that would otherwise distract us from
effectively knowing and serving God. Frugality is similar to sacrifice
and simplicity, yet it is more about recognizing the surplus in our
lives and choosing to stop indulging.

This week will encourage you to reflect on your spending
habits, standard of living, and finances, and it will reveal the
desires of your heart. The goal is to help you experience freedom
from indulgence so you can develop the habit of being more
focused on loving others and walking closely with God.

Heart Test

♥

Fools spend whatever they get.
PROVERBS 21:20

Think about your spending habits.

Do you tend to live above or below your means?

Ask God to help you examine your spending habits this week and what they reveal about the desires of your heart.

What is one practical way you can choose to refrain from using your money today to satisfy a desire?

Could you eat at home instead of eating out?

Not buy something in a store that you probably would have bought if you hadn't read this today?

Do something yourself instead of paying someone else to do it?

Pride Test

♥

Teach those who are rich in this world not to be proud and not to
trust in their money, which is so unreliable. Their trust should
be in God, Who richly gives us all we need for our enjoyment.

1 TIMOTHY 6:17

Shop in places below your usual "standard" this week.

Instead of going to the usual brand-name department stores,
go to a thrift store or secondhand shop.

Buy food at a less expensive store instead of a high-end grocery store.

How easy or difficult is this for you?

Ask the Lord to show you any pride in your heart as you shop,
and then confess that to Him.

Confusing Needs and Wants

♥

Guard against every kind of greed.
Life is not measured by how much you own.
LUKE 12:15

What things do you desire?

A new car? A new pair of shoes? A new couch? A new phone?

Write out a list, and next to each item, indicate whether it is a true need or simply a want.

Next, read the above verse again.

What thoughts and feelings come up as you look at your want/need list?

Take a few moments to talk to God about your list.

Enslaved to Debt

Just as the rich rule the poor,
so the borrower is servant to the lender.
PROVERBS 22:7

Owe nothing to anyone—except for
your obligation to love one another.
ROMANS 13:8

What role does debt play in your life?

"Nothing is a good deal unless you can afford it," states Randy Alcorn in *Managing God's Money*.[20]

If you are in a great amount of debt, make an appointment today to get help from a financial advisor, or see if your church or community offers financial classes.

Ask the Lord if there is anything He might want you to give up now so you can more quickly pay back what you owe.

Entitlement

❤

Those who love money will never have enough.
How meaningless to think that wealth brings true happiness!
ECCLESIASTES 5:10

Reflect honestly before the Lord about any things you feel entitled to.

What do you believe you should not have to give up?

A nice home?

A well-earned vacation?

Eating out at a nice restaurant once a week?

The latest smartphone?

Cable television?

What has influenced how you view these things?

Confess to God any feelings of entitlement and ask yourself if He might be leading you to downsize or eliminate some of your "entitlements."

A Matter of the Heart

♥

What do you benefit if you gain the whole world but lose
your own soul? Is anything worth more than your soul?

MARK 8:36–37

Those who belong to Christ Jesus have nailed the passions and
desires of their sinful nature to His cross and crucified them there.

GALATIANS 5:24

Frugality is one of the most difficult disciplines to practice because it gets to the heart of what most keeps us from God—pride.

How might God be asking you to continue the practice of frugality?

Over the past week, how easy or difficult has it been for you to be frugal? In what areas have you struggled—a desire for pleasure or comfort, pride in thinking of how others might view you, a belief that you can spend your money any way you want, or conviction over debt?

WEEK 45

Rhythms of Rest

♥

[Jesus said,] "Are you tired? Worn out? Burned out on religion?
Come to Me. Get away with Me and you'll recover your life.
I'll show you how to take a real rest. Walk with Me and work
with Me—watch how I do it. Learn the unforced rhythms of grace."
MATTHEW 11:28–30, MSG

In this fast-paced world, rest seems so attractive yet so elusive. However, Jesus doesn't suggest that you rest; He commands it. The practice of rest involves making time to intentionally restore your mind and body for the sake of your soul. Whereas Sabbath rest focuses on setting apart one day each week for rest and worship, this practice focuses on integrating regular rhythms of rest into your day.

These exercises are designed to create intentional moments of rest each day, helping you become more aware of activities, people, and places that restore you, as well as those that drain you. It may feel difficult to allow yourself to truly accept God's invitation to rest. Accepting that your mind, body, and soul need rest means accepting your limitations. Use your limitations as reminders to rest, restore, and reflect on your need for God.

Sit for a Bit

♥

You chart the path ahead of me and tell me where to
stop and rest. Every moment you know where I am.

PSALM 139:3, TLB

Read the verse again, pausing to reflect on each sentence.

What would it feel like to have God tell you to stop and rest?

Can you accept that He actually wants you to do this?

Does rest feel like a gift to enjoy or an imposition in your day?

Do you feel guilty for resting?

Sit right where you are for another five minutes and try to do
nothing but relax your body, quiet your heart before God, and be
open to whatever He might want to say to you.

Restrain Yourself and Rest

There is a special rest still waiting for the people of God.
For all who have entered into God's rest have rested from
their labors, just as God did after creating the world.
HEBREWS 4:9–10

In *24/6: A Prescription for a Healthier, Happier Life*, Matthew Sleeth states, "Rest shows us *who* God is. He has restraint. Restraint is refraining from doing everything that one has the power to do. We must never mistake God's restraint for weakness. The opposite is true. God shows restraint; therefore, restraint is holy."[21]

Think about three areas where you can practice restraint today so you can embrace rest.

For example, you could (1) say no to a social engagement, (2) skip an unnecessary errand, and (3) choose not to take work home.

At the end of the day, talk to God about how it felt to refrain from those activities and to rest.

A Restful Friend

♥

Jesus said, "Let's go off by ourselves to a quiet place and rest awhile."
He said this because there were so many people coming and
going that Jesus and His apostles didn't even have time to eat.
So they left by boat for a quiet place, where they could be alone.

MARK 6:31–32

Is there anyone you know who has the ability to help you slow down and rest?

If so, call or text them today to schedule a time to do something restful and restorative this week.

For example, you could take a walk, play cards, or go out to dinner together.

If you don't know such a person, ask God to send this kind of friend into your life.

A Restful Moment

♥

It is useless for you to work so hard from early morning until late at night,
anxiously working for food to eat; for God gives rest to His loved ones.
PSALM 127:2

Set an alarm on your phone to go off at a random time today. When it does, allow yourself freedom to stop "doing" and just "be" with God—even if only for a minute.

Close your eyes, breathe deeply, clear your mind of all the tasks you need to do, and simply thank God for this brief moment of rest.

Accept God's Gift of Rest

❤

The LORD is my shepherd; I have all that I need. He lets me rest in
green meadows; He leads me beside peaceful streams. He renews my
strength. He guides me along right paths, bringing honor to His name.
PSALM 23:1–3

Sheep are by nature anxious animals.

Unless their shepherd makes them rest, they will continue to
roam until the point of exhaustion.

Read the above verse again, and think about how God might be
inviting you to rest your body today.

It could be through something as small as going for a slow
walk, enjoying a bubble bath, eating a healthy dinner, or going to
bed early.

Embrace this time of rest as a gift from God.

Bring Rest into Your Day

♥

The LORD replied, "I will personally go with you, Moses,
and I will give you rest—everything will be fine for you."

EXODUS 33:14

Take a moment to think about the people and activities that fill the day ahead.

Next, read the verse again, but replace Moses' name with your own, as if God were speaking these words directly to you.

End this time by taking a few deep breaths.

Imagine breathing in God's presence and exhaling your anxiety and fears for the day ahead.

As you end your week of "rest" exercises, think back to which ones really helped you rest.

Ask God how He might like you to integrate them into your life's regular rhythm over the next several weeks.

WEEK 46

Heart Problems

♥

I fear that somehow your pure and undivided devotion to Christ will be
corrupted, just as Eve was deceived by the cunning ways of the serpent.

2 CORINTHIANS 11:3

Which sins most tempt you? Are you aware of when you are most
vulnerable to Satan's attacks? Wherever you are most susceptible
to temptation is where you will discover a "heart problem." In the
Bible, the heart is considered the center of thought and feeling. God
cautions us to guard the heart above all else, because it determines
the course of our lives (see Proverbs 4:23). Therefore, one of the
most important things we can do is to watch over it closely. The
practice of "guarding your heart," also called "watchfulness," is
being alert to Satan's temptations.

These exercises will help you grow in self-awareness, which
is essential if you are to withstand being blindsided by the enemy.
Self-awareness alone is not enough to produce watchfulness. You
need to ask for help from the Holy Spirit and godly friends. Ask
the Lord to help you be proactive in your battle for those places in
your heart most vulnerable to the enemy's attacks.

First and Last Thoughts

♥

"Why are you sleeping?" He asked them.
"Get up and pray, so that you will not give in to temptation."
LUKE 22:46

Over the next week, write down what thoughts enter your mind when you first wake up and as you go to sleep.

Are these thoughts mostly centered on yourself and your agenda?

Do you think much about God and how you can align your heart with His?

Put a note by your bed right now, reminding you to make your last thoughts today about God and to guard your heart throughout the day tomorrow.

Now refer back to February 7 to see your thoughts on this same exercise.

How have your thoughts or desires changed over the past year? Do you notice any new sin tendencies?

Knowing Your Weak Spots

♥

We are familiar with his evil schemes.
2 CORINTHIANS 2:11

In *Journey with Jesus*, spiritual director Larry Warner asserts that an evil spirit sent by Satan is a "brilliant military commander, who will attack you again and again at two points: your personal weakness and places of internal complacency."[22]

Do you know where you are most vulnerable to temptation? Are you familiar with how Satan likes to tempt you in these areas?

If not, take note of where your mind often tends to drift. Since Satan knows your weak spots, make every effort to know them as well so you can defend yourself against his attacks.

Today, ask God and a trusted friend where your weak spots are. Be willing to be open to what you hear. Then whenever you find yourself tempted in those areas, pray instead, asking God to rule over your mind and heart.

Words That Defeat Temptation

♥

Jesus was led by the Spirit into the wilderness to be tempted there by the devil. For forty days and forty nights He fasted and became very hungry. During that time the devil came and said to Him, "If You are the Son of God, tell these stones to become loaves of bread." But Jesus told him, "No! The Scriptures say, 'People do not live by bread alone, but by every word that comes from the mouth of God.'"

MATTHEW 4:1-4

Based on Jesus' responses to Satan's temptations, scholars believe that during His time in the wilderness, Jesus had been meditating on the book of Deuteronomy.

After learning more about your own sin tendencies, choose one Scripture to write out and place it where you will frequently see it.

This will help your mind stay focused on God's Word during times of temptation.

To Whom Are You Listening?

♥

"You won't die!" the serpent replied to the woman. "God knows that your eyes will be opened as soon as you eat it, and you will be like God, knowing both good and evil." The woman was convinced. She saw that the tree was beautiful and its fruit looked delicious, and she wanted the wisdom it would give her. So she took some of the fruit and ate it.

GENESIS 3:4-6

God's voice is always loving, kind, and patient. Satan's voice is contradictory to God's—demeaning, accusatory, and demanding.

Take a moment to be still before the Lord.

Now think about the kinds of thoughts that occupy your mind throughout the day.

Are they God's words, yours, or the enemy's?

Emotional Attacks

Guard your heart above all else,
for it determines the course of your life.
PROVERBS 4:23

Preacher Charles Stanley once stated, "Disappointment is inevitable. But to become discouraged, there's a choice I make. God would never discourage me. He would always point me to Himself to trust Him. Therefore, my discouragement is from Satan. As you go through the emotions that we have, hostility is not from God, bitterness, unforgiveness, all of these are attacks from Satan."[23]

How might Satan be attacking you through your emotions?

Are you experiencing discouragement? Hostility? Bitterness? Unforgiveness? Self-loathing?

Confess these things to God to break their power over your heart.

Be Careful …

♥

If you think you are standing strong, be careful not to fall. The temptations in your life are no different from what others experience. And God is faithful. He will not allow the temptation to be more than you can stand. When you are tempted, He will show you a way out so that you can endure.

1 CORINTHIANS 10:12–13

What sin do you feel you have conquered or have moved beyond?

Prayerfully read the verses again.

What comes to mind as you read them?

How might this sin come back to catch you unaware?

End today by praying the Jesus Prayer: "Jesus Christ, Son of God, have mercy on me, a sinner."

(For a reminder of the Jesus Prayer, refer back to August 5.)

WEEK 47

NOV. 19

Give Thanks

♥

I will offer you a sacrifice of thanksgiving
and call on the name of the Lord.
PSALM 116:17

Give thanks to the Lord, for He is good!
His faithful love endures forever.
1 CHRONICLES 16:34

There have probably been days, months, or even years when you've had more than your fair share of suffering. But being thankful can actually help you in difficult times by changing the way you look at life. Complaining connects you to your unhappiness—gratitude connects you to the source of real joy. Expressing gratitude to God is actually a form of worship. Similarly, you honor others when you thank them, respecting them for who they are and what they have done. There may be times when it feels hard to find something to be thankful for. Ask God to open your heart to His blessings in your life—those right in front of you and those that have not yet unfolded. This attitude of gratitude will allow you to see life as a gift to enjoy instead of a burden to bear.

Daily Gifts

♥

This is the day the LORD has made.
We will rejoice and be glad in it.
PSALM 118:24

Set an alert on your phone for every day this week to remind you to ask yourself, "What can I thank God for today?"

When the alarm goes off, take a moment to thank God for whatever gifts come to mind—another day of life, family, a roof over your head, a smile someone gave you, an encouraging word you heard, or owning a Bible without fear of being persecuted.

The more you look for those things, the more you'll discover that you have many things to be grateful for.

Surprised by Gratitude

♥

Always be joyful. Never stop praying.
Be thankful in all circumstances, for this is
God's will for you who belong to Christ Jesus.
1 THESSALONIANS 5:16-18

In retrospect, what is something you could have been thankful for at the time it was happening, but you weren't?

For example, you might now be thankful God worked out good through a bad experience, or you might be thankful you went through a difficult time because it caused you to learn a lot.

Does this realization surprise you?

What is something you are not thankful for right now?

Might this be something for which you will be thankful when you look back months or years from now?

Thank God for the work He is currently doing, which you will someday recognize and appreciate.

Your Work in Progress

❤

Be strong and immovable. Always work enthusiastically for the Lord,
for you know that nothing you do for the Lord is ever useless.
1 CORINTHIANS 15:58

Whether you work in or outside the home, how can you thank God for the work in your day?

Are you thankful for your coworkers?

Your boss?

Your commute?

Your paycheck?

Being able to stay home with your children?

Being physically able to do household chores?

Thank God for these things and ask Him to give you strength to work enthusiastically for Him today.

Gratitude for Answered Prayers

Keep on asking, and you will receive what you ask for.
Keep on seeking, and you will find.
Keep on knocking, and the door will be opened to you.
For everyone who asks, receives. Everyone who seeks, finds.
And to everyone who knocks, the door will be opened.

MATTHEW 7:7-8

All too often, we pray and pray and then forget to thank God when He answers us!

Has God recently answered a persistent prayer of yours?

Take a moment to remember how you received what you asked for, and then thank Him for it!

Gratitude Set to Music

♥

Be filled with the Holy Spirit, singing psalms and
hymns and spiritual songs among yourselves,
and making music to the Lord in your hearts.
And give thanks for everything to God the
Father in the name of our Lord Jesus Christ.

EPHESIANS 5:18–20

Make music to the Lord in your heart today by giving Him
thanks.

Choose a hymn or spiritual song to sing or play throughout
your day (in your car, in the shower, as you do dishes, as you go
for a run, etc.).

Listen to the words as you worship, and allow them to lead
your heart to praise God for who He is and what He has done for
you.

Beautiful Gratitude

♥

O LORD, what a variety of things You have made!
In wisdom You have made them all.
The earth is full of Your creatures.
Here is the ocean, vast and wide, teeming
with life of every kind, both large and small.
PSALM 104:24-25

Poet Ralph Waldo Emerson stated, "Never lose an opportunity for seeing anything that is beautiful; for beauty is God's hand-writing—a wayside sacrament. Welcome it in every fair face, in every fair sky, in every fair flower, and thank God for it as a cup of blessing."[24]

Look for something beautiful and take a picture of it to remind you to thank God for blessing your life with beauty today.

How have these exercises in thankfulness impacted the way you think, feel, and live?

Have you noticed any improvement in your attitude as you practiced gratitude?

WEEK 48

NOV. 26

Let Go to Save Your Life

♥

If you cling to your life, you will lose it,
and if you let your life go, you will save it.

LUKE 17:33

At first glance, Jesus' words seem like a paradox. But they make sense when you think about letting something go before grasping something else.

The practice of "letting go" is releasing your grip on anything that has taken God's place in your life. Not only does it help build trust in God, but it eventually results in true freedom.

You are free when you no longer need anyone or anything besides God for your fulfillment, satisfaction, or identity. This is what Jesus meant when He said, "The truth will set you free" (John 8:32).

The exercises this week will help you recognize and confess the attachments that make you a slave to this world so you can rebuild your trust in God alone.

Give yourself grace this week, remembering that the hard choice to "let go" is one you will need to make over and over again.

The Paradox of Control

❤

Those who love their life in this world will lose it.
Those who care nothing for their life in
this world will keep it for eternity.
JOHN 12:25

Where is it difficult for you to let go? Ask a close friend or family member for their opinion.

Do you feel a need to control the day's activities?

Do you try to control everything about your future?

How about your desires for your family?

Do you need to let go of anger or bitterness that you have held on to for a long time?

Ask God to show you how to begin letting go of this thing over the next week so you can be free from its control over you.

Out of Your Hands

♥

Give all your worries and cares to God, for He cares about you.
1 PETER 5:7

Practice the following prayer of "letting go."

Begin by opening your hands with your palms facing up. With your hands still out, tell God the things that are hard for you to trust Him with today.

A relationship?

A work situation?

All the things you need to get done?

When you are finished praying, flip your hands over to symbolize "letting go" of these issues into God's care.

If those worries come up again throughout the day, remind yourself that you already let go of them and placed them in God's care.

Can You Give It Up?

❤

"I've obeyed all these commandments," the young man replied.
"What else must I do?" Jesus told him, "If you want to be perfect,
go and sell all your possessions and give the money to the poor,
and you will have treasure in heaven. Then come, follow Me."
But when the young man heard this, he went away sad, for he had
many possessions. Then Jesus said to His disciples, "I tell you the truth,
it is very hard for a rich person to enter the Kingdom of Heaven."

MATTHEW 19:20-23

Practice "letting go" this week by giving away something you are attached to.

Perhaps it is a possession, your time, or your space.

Take a few moments to pray silently and ask the Lord to bring something to mind.

How can you begin the process of letting it go?

Out with the Old

———— ♥ ————

My old self has been crucified with Christ.
It is no longer I who live, but Christ lives in me.
So I live in this earthly body by trusting in the
Son of God, Who loved me and gave Himself for me.

GALATIANS 2:20

What parts of your "old self" might God be calling you to let go of?

Anger?

Sin habits?

An attachment to image?

A need to be the best?

Confess these things to God and ask Him to help you let go of them so you can center your identity on the truth that you are loved by Him.

The Loss of Letting Go

♥

When Mary arrived and saw Jesus, she fell at his feet and said, "Lord, if only You had been here, my brother would not have died." When Jesus saw her weeping and saw the other people wailing with her, a deep anger welled up within Him, and He was deeply troubled. "Where have you put him?" He asked them. They told Him, "Lord, come and see." Then Jesus wept. The people who were standing nearby said, "See how much He loved him!"

JOHN 11:32–36

Letting go can feel like a loss.

Read the above passage again and think about Jesus weeping with those He loves.

What have you recently let go of that grieves you?

How does Jesus weep with you in this loss?

The Greatest Love

❤

> After breakfast Jesus asked Simon Peter,
> "Simon son of John, do you love Me more than these?"
> **JOHN 21:15**

Imagine Jesus asking you this same question: "(Insert your name), do you love Me more than these?"

Whenever you have trouble letting go of something, this is an indicator that you love it more than Jesus.

Over the past several days, what has been hardest for you to let go of?

What loves have replaced your love for Jesus?

Confess this to the Lord, asking Him to change your heart so that He is your first love.

WEEK 49

Reasons to Celebrate

Enter His gates with thanksgiving; go into His courts
with praise. Give thanks to Him and praise His name.
For the LORD is good. His unfailing love continues forever,
and His faithfulness continues to each generation.

PSALM 100:4-5

We celebrate anniversaries, birthdays, victories, promotions, milestones, marriages, and new babies. We also celebrate occasions such as the Lord's Supper and baptism. The ultimate reason to celebrate is that God has rescued us from the consequences of sin and shown us the wonders of eternity. Celebration is a powerful tool to take our focus off our troubles and put it on God's blessings, and ultimately on God Himself. Those who love Him truly have the most to celebrate!

The exercises this week will awaken you to things worth celebrating. Some may seem insignificant, but think of them as small steps to incorporate a spirit of celebration into daily life. These enjoyable experiences are a tiny taste of the joyous celebrations you will experience in eternity. Feel the freedom to laugh with God and others, delight in the ordinary, and live with a spirit of thankfulness that God wants you to celebrate!

Celebrate Routine Accomplishments

♥

The master said, "Well done, my good and faithful servant.
You have been faithful in handling this small amount, so now I will
give you many more responsibilities. Let's celebrate together!"
MATTHEW 25:23

Celebration gives you the opportunity to savor the joy of work, creates a spirit of gratitude, and renews your energy for the work still to be done.

To open your heart to the practice of celebration, think of one thing that you routinely accomplish every day but have never thought to celebrate—putting a good meal on the table, going to work every day, paying your bills, or tucking the kids into bed.

Celebrate one of these daily accomplishments by doing something you enjoy.

For example, go out with your spouse or a friend for dinner or maybe just relax by the fire with a good book.

The Ultimate Celebration

❦

After this I saw a vast crowd, too great to count, from every nation
and tribe and people and language, standing in front of the throne
and before the Lamb. They were clothed in white robes and held
palm branches in their hands. And they were shouting with a great roar,
"Salvation comes from our God who sits on the throne and from the Lamb!"
And all the angels were standing around the throne and around
the elders and the four living beings. And they fell before
the throne with their faces to the ground and worshiped God.

REVELATION 7:9-11

Read the passage again, but this time imagine yourself in this ultimate celebration scene.

What feelings come up as you look around you?

As you see God on His throne?

What can you do today to celebrate that this will one day be a reality?

A Person to Celebrate

—— ♥ ——

"Kill the calf we have been fattening. We must celebrate
with a feast, for this son of mine was dead and has now returned
to life. He was lost, but now he is found." So the party began.

LUKE 15:23–24

Ask God to put on your mind a person who would benefit if you
celebrated them this week.

Take them to lunch, buy them a small gift, or write them a
letter simply to say that they are valuable to God and to you and
are therefore worth celebrating.

A New Way to Celebrate

❤

David danced before the Lᴏʀᴅ with all
his might, wearing a priestly garment.
2 SAMUEL 6:14

We can serve God, not in the old way of obeying the
letter of the law, but in the new way of living in the Spirit.
ROMANS 7:6

Celebrate God in a new way this week.

For example, you may want to dance to worship music, attend
a worship service that isn't necessarily your style, or praise God
out in nature.

What is it like for you to engage in a different type of celebration
than what you are used to?

From Trouble to Celebration

♥

For the despondent, every day brings trouble;
for the happy heart, life is a continual feast.
PROVERBS 15:15

Rather than focusing today on your present troubles, choose something small to celebrate instead—such as having your needs met, seeing a change in the weather, or enjoying a free night with family.

Celebrate this in a way that sets it apart from everyday life.

For example, have friends over for dinner, go out for ice cream, or buy something small to remind you to celebrate the little things more often.

Celebrating You

♥

The LORD your God is living among you. He is a mighty savior.
He will take delight in you with gladness. With His love, He will
calm all your fears. He will rejoice over you with joyful songs.
ZEPHANIAH 3:17

What do you think God is celebrating about you?

Perhaps that you trusted Him through a hard season, enjoyed a particular moment more, responded to a difficult situation with grace, loved someone well, were faithful to read His Word?

How has this past week encouraged you to celebrate the victories and blessings in your life with God?

WEEK 50

Hide His Words in Your Heart

I have hidden Your word in my heart, that I might not sin against You.
PSALM 119:11

Increased access to information through the internet is making memorization a lost art. However, the Bible states that something important happens in your heart when you meditate and memorize God's Word. The Lord wants you to store up His Word in your heart (Psalm 119:11), apply your heart to learning His Word (Proverbs 3:1-2), and commit yourself wholeheartedly to living by His Word (Deuteronomy 11:18). When you practice memorization through repetition and reflection, it shapes your mind and heart into a closer reflection of God's image and character.

The exercises this week will focus on memorizing just one verse, an Old Testament prophecy of the coming Messiah. Each day has a small section of the verse to think deeply about and commit to memory. If memorizing is difficult for you, give yourself grace. It may take you longer than a week to memorize a verse, and that is okay. What you commit to memory will always be with you, regardless of whether or not Wi-Fi is available.

A Child Is Born to Us

♥

A Child is born to us, a Son is given to us.
The government will rest on His shoulders.
And He will be called: Wonderful Counselor,
Mighty God, Everlasting Father, Prince of Peace.
ISAIAH 9:6, EMPHASIS ADDED

Read the whole verse once.

Now read it again, but this time read it slowly.

Memorize the italicized words of this verse.

Picture Jesus coming into the world as a small, helpless child.

Try to repeat these words throughout the day to solidify them in your memory.

A Son Is Given to Us

♥

A Child is born to us, *a Son is given to us.*
The government will rest on His shoulders.
And He will be called: Wonderful Counselor,
Mighty God, Everlasting Father, Prince of Peace.
ISAIAH 9:6, EMPHASIS ADDED

Write the entire verse and post it in a place where you can read it often—such as on your bathroom mirror, at the kitchen sink, or on your bedside table.

Repeat the section you memorized yesterday and then memorize the italicized words for today.

Reflect on what it must have felt like for God to give us His Son.

The Government Will Rest on His Shoulders

A Child is born to us, a Son is given to us.
The government will rest on His shoulders.
And He will be called: Wonderful Counselor,
Mighty God, Everlasting Father, Prince of Peace.
ISAIAH 9:6, EMPHASIS ADDED

Repeat several times what you have memorized so far.

Next, slowly read the italicized section for today.

Imagine the government being led by someone who is absolutely wise, loving, and caring, who treats all people equally, and who rules with perfect justice.

It's hard to wrap our minds around what it would be like to live in a country with a leader who could do those wonderful things.

Rejoice and thank God that someday this will be a reality for the whole world.

Wonderful Counselor

———— ♥ ————

A Child is born to us, a Son is given to us.
The government will rest on His shoulders.
And He will be called: Wonderful Counselor,
Mighty God, Everlasting Father, Prince of Peace.

ISAIAH 9:6, EMPHASIS ADDED

————————————

Repeat several times what you have memorized so far.

Then read the italicized section for today and reflect on the words *Wonderful Counselor*.

How often do you seek Jesus out as your counselor for wisdom, advice, and discernment?

How have you experienced Him as a Wonderful Counselor?

Take a moment to reflect on this as you memorize today's section of the verse.

Mighty God

♥

A Child is born to us, a Son is given to us.
The government will rest on His shoulders.
And He will be called: Wonderful Counselor,
Mighty God, Everlasting Father, Prince of Peace.
ISAIAH 9:6, EMPHASIS ADDED

Repeat what you have memorized so far and memorize the next italicized section for today.

Often we think of Jesus only as gentle and kind. But He will return as a mighty warrior to defeat evil forever.

Think about times when Jesus has proven Himself to be mighty in your life.

How do you need Him to be mighty right now?

Everlasting Father, Prince of Peace

♥

A Child is born to us, a Son is given to us.
The government will rest on His shoulders.
And He will be called: Wonderful Counselor,
Mighty God, *Everlasting Father, Prince of Peace.*
ISAIAH 9:6, EMPHASIS ADDED

Repeat the verse several times *slowly*. Allow its truth to sink in as you recite these words.

Now read and memorize the final italicized section. Reflect on Jesus being an Everlasting Father and think about living under a perfect ruler for eternity.

Reflect on Jesus as the Prince of Peace and imagine living in a place where there will be no wars or conflict with others.

End the time by reciting from memory the entire passage of Isaiah 9:6.

How has memorizing this verse prepared your heart to celebrate Jesus in a fresh way?

WEEK 51

DEC. 17

Pause and Reflect

♥

Keep putting into practice all you learned and received
from me—everything you heard from me and saw
me doing. Then the God of peace will be with you.

PHILIPPIANS 4:9

In a world that pressures you to keep moving, reflection helps you pause and remember how God has worked in and around you.

The end of the year is the perfect time to reflect with the Lord on what has happened and what you learned. Think about the victories and hardships of this past year and be attentive to how God might use them to guide and direct you into the new year.

Because it is difficult to deeply reflect over an entire year and a new year in just seven days, this practice is stretched into two weeks. The first week focuses on looking back at what God has done in your life over the past year. The second week focuses on how God might be leading you as you enter into a new year.

May God bless you and give you peace as you continue to put into practice all you have learned.

Reflecting on Your Growth

♥

I remember the days of old. I ponder all Your
great works and think about what You have done.
PSALM 143:5

As you have walked with God through the spiritual practices in
this devotional, was there one practice in particular that helped
you grow the most?

Write down some examples of when you noticed growth. Be
as specific as you can.

End today by thanking God for His work in your life.

Throwing Off the Old, Putting On the New

❤

Throw off your old sinful nature and your former way of life,
which is corrupted by lust and deception. Instead, let the Spirit
renew your thoughts and attitudes. Put on your new nature,
created to be like God--truly righteous and holy.

EPHESIANS 4:22-24

What was one of the hardest truths God showed you about yourself over the past year?

Was there a specific practice that challenged you the most?

Take five or ten minutes to think about this and come up with one possible reason for why this was the area in which you needed to be challenged.

Life-Giving Words

❤

Such things were written in the Scriptures long ago to teach us.
And the Scriptures give us hope and encouragement as
we wait patiently for God's promises to be fulfilled.

ROMANS 15:4

What is the best word of advice or encouragement from Scripture you received this past year?

Write this verse or phrase down and put it in a visible spot this week to help you reflect on how God is faithful to encourage us through His Word.

Divine Appointment

♥

You Philippians were the only ones who gave me financial help when
I first brought you the Good News and then traveled on from Macedonia.
No other church did this. Even when I was in Thessalonica you sent
help more than once.... At the moment I have all I need—and more!
I am generously supplied with the gifts you sent me with Epaphroditus.
They are a sweet-smelling sacrifice that is acceptable and pleasing to God.

PHILIPPIANS 4:15-16, 18

Whom did God put into your life at just the right moment this
past year?

Thank God for how He provides for you.

The Pleasures of God

♥

You will show me the way of life, granting me the joy of
Your presence and the pleasures of living with You forever.

PSALM 16:11

I will sing to the LORD because He is good to me.

PSALM 13:6

What is one of the happiest moments you shared with the Lord
over the past year?

Take a moment to reflect on that special time with Him.

What did this experience teach you about who God is?

Choose Not to Be Afraid

♥

The Lord is my light and my salvation—so why should I be afraid?
PSALM 27:1

The Lord is for me, so I will have no fear.
What can mere people do to me?
PSALM 118:6

Fear paralyzes; courage releases you to move forward.

The Bible speaks of the courage to stand firm against evil, to remain strong in your faith, to resist temptation, to do the right thing, to confidently hope that God will work good in your life.

Where did you grow most in courage this past year?

WEEK 52

DEC. 24

The Greatest Gift

Praise the Lord ... because He has visited and
redeemed His people. He has sent us a mighty Savior.

LUKE 1:68-69

There is a great difference between Adam's sin and God's
gracious gift. For the sin of this one man, Adam, brought death
to many. But even greater is God's wonderful grace and His gift
of forgiveness to many through this other man, Jesus Christ.

ROMANS 5:15

Whatever is good and perfect is a gift coming down to us
from God our Father, Who created all the lights in the heavens.

JAMES 1:17

This week, we'll look ahead to next year, holding on to what we've
learned and practiced while considering how we can keep those
habits alive and strong. In order to do that, first think about this
important question: What was the greatest gift God gave you this
past year?

Carry It Forward

My child, never forget the things I have taught you.
Store My commands in your heart. If you do this,
you will live many years, and your life will be satisfying.
PROVERBS 3:1-2

I am certain that God, who began the good work
within you, will continue His work until it is finally
finished on the day when Christ Jesus returns.
PHILIPPIANS 1:6

What is one new thing you learned this year that you look forward
to carrying into the next year?

Who Is Doing Your Planning for Next Year?

Look here, you who say, "Today or tomorrow we are going
to a certain town and will stay there a year. We will do
business there and make a profit." How do you know
what your life will be like tomorrow? … What you
ought to say is, "If the Lord wants us to, we will live
and do this or that." Otherwise you are boasting about
your own pretentious plans, and all such boasting is evil.

JAMES 4:13–16

What plans have you already made for the new year?

Write your three biggest goals.

Now draw three blank lines below those goals.

Pull out this paper at the end of next year to see if you can fill
in those lines with plans God had for you that you hadn't foreseen.

Always Learning

♥

I know the LORD is always with me.
I will not be shaken, for He is right beside me.
PSALM 16:8

God has made everything beautiful for its own time.
He has planted eternity in the human heart, but even so,
people cannot see the whole scope of God's
work from beginning to end.
ECCLESIASTES 3:11

I will lead blind Israel down a new path, guiding them
along an unfamiliar way. I will brighten the darkness
before them and smooth out the road ahead of them.
Yes, I will indeed do these things; I will not forsake them.
ISAIAH 42:16

What hard experience from this past year are you still learning
to trust God with? What do you think He is trying to teach you
through it? In what ways can you use the practices you've learned
to help you trust God?

Don't Sweat the Details

———— ♥ ————

Her sister, Mary, sat at the Lord's feet, listening to what He taught.
But Martha was distracted by the big dinner she was preparing....
"Lord, doesn't it seem unfair to you that my sister just sits here while
I do all the work? Tell her to come and help me." But the Lord said to her,
"My dear Martha, you are worried and upset over all these details!"

LUKE 10:39-41

———————————————————————

What details and distractions keep you from being present with others and with God?

As you head into the new year, consider one way to let your expectations go regarding how your home or appearance "should" be.

For example, don't pick up your child's toys until the end of the day.

Ask God to remind you that loving others well is more about your presence than about your presentation.

Prayer for the New Year

— ❤ —

Your Father already knows your needs. Seek the Kingdom of God above
all else, and He will give you everything you need. So don't be afraid, little
flock. For it gives your Father great happiness to give you the Kingdom.

LUKE 12:30-32

Write down a prayer for the new year.

It can be about anything—a prayer for someone close to you,
a prayer for growth, or a prayer for the healing of a relationship.

Keep this prayer and reread it on the first of each month to see
how God continues to work in this situation.

To Do or Not to Do

♥

For everything there is a season, a time for every activity under heaven.
ECCLESIASTES 3:1

Take a few moments to write down your primary commitments from this past year.

Be specific. For example, don't just say "church" but list all the different ways you were involved there.

Pray through each one and ask the Lord if there is anything He is asking you to let go of or add to your list for the next year.

Spend time quietly listening for His voice.

From This Day Forward

— ♥ —

Remember the things I have done in the past. For I alone am God! I am God, and there is none like Me. Only I can tell you the future before it even happens. Everything I plan will come to pass, for I do whatever I wish.

ISAIAH 46:9–10

Keep putting into practice all you learned and received from me—everything you heard from me and saw me doing. Then the God of peace will be with you.

PHILIPPIANS 4:9

What things are you already anticipating or anxious about for this next year?

Offer these things to the Lord as you read the Scriptures again. Ask Him to help you be present with Him in each of these moments.

Then look back over all the spiritual practices you worked through. Ask God which one or two practices He would like you to continue working on.

ADDITIONAL RESOURCES

♥

The additional books listed below will help you continue your growth as you develop the spiritual practices you've learned.

May God give you the strength and motivation to continue exercising your spiritual muscles this next year. May you develop more habits of the heart that will help you grow in your faith and keep you walking close to him.

Spiritual Disciplines Handbook:
Practices That Transform Us by Adele Calhoun
Celebration of Discipline by Richard Foster
Practicing Basic Spiritual Disciplines by Charles Stanley
The Spirit of the Disciplines by Dallas Willard
Renovation of the Heart by Dallas Willard

ACKNOWLEDGMENTS

♥

Thank you to the most wonderful, insightful, and caring professors and mentors—John Coe, Betsy Barber, and Judy Tenelshof. So much of this book is based off the things you taught me!

Thank you, Larry Warner and Jackie Sevier, for being my spiritual directors and continually pointing me back to Christ.

Thank you, Ron and Becki Beers, for countless hours of editing and, most importantly, for raising me to know and love the Lord.

And my biggest thanks goes to my husband, Stetson. Thank you for the countless hours you sat with me to brainstorm, process, and pray for this devotional. Thank you for the early mornings you took our girls so that I could write. Thank you for loving me and cheering me on until the very end.

ABOUT THE AUTHOR

Katherine Butler was first introduced to spiritual formation as an undergraduate at Biola University.

There she attended a special program for a small number of students and faculty, where they lived together at a retreat house for several weeks, studying the topic of spiritual formation and practicing spiritual disciplines within community.

It was during that time that Katy felt her heart awakened to know God deeply and to feel loved and known by Him in return. This experience led her to pursue a master's degree in spiritual formation and soul care from Talbot Seminary in Southern California, where she also became a certified spiritual director.

Katy is passionate about walking with others as they learn more about who God has created them to be. She believes God works with each of His children in ways that are special and unique to them.

Her desire is to help others open themselves to a greater awareness of God's deep and faithful love for them and His presence in their everyday lives.

Katy lives in Illinois with her husband and two beautiful little girls.

NOTES

1. C. S. Lewis, *Letters to Malcolm: Chiefly on Prayer*, quoted in *The Quotable Lewis*, eds. Wayne Martindale and Jerry Root (Carol Stream, IL: Tyndale, 2012), 255.

2. Bill Gaultiere, "Dallas Willard's One Word for Jesus," *Soul Shepherding*, June 11, 2008, http://www.soulshepherding.org/2008/06/dallas-willards-one-word-for-jesus/.

3. A. W. Tozer, *The Knowledge of the Holy* (San Francisco: HarperOne, 1961), 1.

4. John Calvin, *Institutes of the Christian Religion*, trans. Henry Beveridge (Peabody, MA: Hendrickson Publishers, 2008), 4.

5. Tim Keller, Twitter, October 11, 2013, https://twitter.com/dailykeller/status/388624900111335424?lang=en.

6. Lee Strobel, *God's Outrageous Claims* (Grand Rapids, MI: Zondervan, 1998), 23.

7. C. S. Lewis, *The Great Divorce* (San Francisco: HarperOne, 2015), 75.

8. Dallas Willard, *Hearing God* (Downers Grove, IL: IVP, 2012), 218.

9. Ann Voskamp, "When Your Plans Don't Turn Out at All—What Turns Out to Be the Actual Case," *Ann Voskamp* (blog), July 6, 2015, http://annvoskamp.com/2015/07/when-your-plans-dont-turn-out-at-all-what-turns-out-to-be-the-actual-case/.

10. C. S. Lewis, *Reflections on the Psalms* (New York: Harcourt, Brace & Co., 1958), 97.

11. Dallas Willard, *The Spirit of the Disciplines* (San Francisco: Harper-SanFrancisco, 1988), 177.

12. Randy Alcorn, *The Treasure Principle* (Colorado Springs: Multnomah, 2001), 71.

13. Henri Nouwen, *Here and Now* (New York: Crossroad Publishing, 1994), 18.

14. Joshua Lujan Loveless, "Eugene Peterson on Being a Real Pastor," *Relevant*, June 7, 2011, http://www.relevantmagazine.com/next/blog/6-main-slideshow/1262-eugene-peterson-on-being-a-real-pastor.

15. Corrie ten Boom, quoted in Max Lucado, *Life to the Full* (Nashville: Thomas Nelson, 2005), 48.

16. C. S. Lewis, *The Weight of Glory* (San Francisco, HarperOne, 1949), 160.

17. P. Doddridge, *The Works of the Rev. P. Doddridge, D. D.*, vol. 3 (Leeds: Edward Baines, 1803), 485.

18. Richard Foster, *Prayer* (San Francisco: HarperSanFrancisco, 1992), 147.

19. Jen Wilkin, "Choose Hospitality," Proverbs 31 Ministries, January 19, 2016, http://proverbs31.org/devotions/devo/choose-hospitality/.

20. Randy Alcorn, *Managing God's Money* (Carol Stream, IL: Tyndale, 2011), 173.

21. Matthew Sleeth, *24/6: A Prescription for a Healthier, Happier Life* (Carol Stream, IL: Tyndale, 2012), 33.

22. Larry Warner, *Journey with Jesus* (Downers Grove, IL: IVP, 2010), 115.

23. "Charles Stanley: Satan 'Always Attacks the Mind,'" beliefnet, accessed January 4, 2017, http://www.beliefnet.com/faiths/christianity/2004/10/charles-stanley-satan-always-attacks-the-mind.aspx#rmdxLyUCShY8QgV7.99.

24. Ralph Waldo Emerson, quoted in Helen Granat, *Wisdom Through the Ages* (Poulsbo, WA: Miklen Press, 1998), 21.